WITHDRAWN

MUSIC AND CRITICISM
A SYMPOSIUM

LONDON : GEOFFREY CUMBERLEGE

OXFORD UNIVERSITY PRESS

MUSIC

AND

CRITICISM

A SYMPOSIUM

EDITED BY

RICHARD F. FRENCH

HARVARD UNIVERSITY PRESS

Cambridge, Massachusetts

1948

NORWOOD PRESS
J. S. CUSHING CO.; BERWICK AND SMITH CO.;
C. B. FLEMING & CO.
NORWOOD, MASSACHUSETTS, U.S.A.

71831

PREFACE

The addresses which appear in this small volume were delivered at a Symposium on Music Criticism, held at Harvard University, Cambridge, Massachusetts, during the first three days of May, 1947. The meetings and concerts of the Symposium were attended by more than eight hundred guests of the University, representing a variety of musical professions and interests, who came to Cambridge from more than forty states. The Symposium was conceived, formulated, and executed under the direction of Professor A. Tillman Merritt, Chairman of the Department of Music in Harvard University, and was financed through the generosity of Mrs. A. W. Erickson, Mr. and Mrs. John Nicholas Brown, Professor Walter Piston, and the Elizabeth Sprague Coolidge Foundation in the Library of Congress. For further advice and assistance, the Department of Music is indebted to Provost Paul H. Buck, to the curators of the Lucius W. Nieman Foundation, to Professors Theodore Spencer, Paul Sachs, and Harry Levin, and to Mr. William Pinkerton of the Harvard University News Office.

It is tempting to allow these papers to speak for themselves, to refrain from any comment whatsoever. Professor Davison's introductory remarks reveal the feeling of the Department that "someone ought to do something about music criticism," and the titles of the addresses, which were selected by the Department to be delivered in the order in which they appear in this volume, indicate the topics which the Department felt could be treated to advantage in such a series of meetings. The papers of Mr. Forster and Mr. Sessions were to deal with critical problems of a general and philosophical nature; those of Mr. Wind, Mme Samaroff, and Mr. Thomson were to take as their point of departure the discussion of individual works of art from the standpoint of the creator, the interpreter, and the audience; and those of Mr. Kinkeldey, Mr. Lang, and Mr. Cairns were to treat technical matters of immediate importance. The reader should bear in mind, however, that the Symposium was conceived not as a sequence of meetings which would give final answers to difficult questions, but as the initial impulse to a succession of thoughts and actions which might contribute to the effectiveness of the music critic in our musical life. This was the specific purpose of the Symposium, and it is worth a preface to state it in plain language because by so doing, attention can be drawn to at least three ideas which are engagingly and disastrously easy to infer:

First, that the well-trained music critic is the panacea for all our musical ills. This is patent nonsense. The music critic can be effective only in so far as he is a useful member of a society which wants and uses music; and though a discussion of music in our society can be approached from the standpoint of the duties and responsibilities of the music critic, the discussion becomes abstract and futile if it fails to consider all the other factors—musical and non-musical—which affect those duties and responsibilities and vice versa. The composer, the scientist, and the businessman, to name only three and to understate the case, are of equal importance with the critic in directing a satisfactory musical expression.

Second, that the music critic can find in these papers a resolution of all his difficulties. This is precisely what he cannot find, search as he will. What he may come upon is a series of ideas and observations which may help him to think more clearly about his profession. But thinking is only a portion of his lot. It is precisely at the point where the critic needs the greatest help—at the point where he must bring all his thought to bear upon his daily life—that these papers are of the least value. The responsibility for this inadequacy is entirely that of the Department of Music, which selected both the subjects and the speakers, and I emphasize it only because it illuminates (among other things) one whole area—the field within which the critic must exercise his practical responsibilities—which (with the exception of Mme Samaroff's paper) was touched upon only in most cursory and unsatisfactory fashion at the afternoon discussion sessions. If other institutions are moved to continue the investigation of critical problems, this is an area within which they could with profit concentrate their efforts.

Third, that institutions of higher education are necessarily the instruments best fitted to sponsor a Symposium of this sort. I wish I could support this inference, but I cannot. I mean specifically that at the present time there are very few, if any, Departments of Music or Schools of Music whose faculties enjoy historical perspective combined with a knowledge of the actual to a degree which qualifies them to deal intelligently with this and a host of other musical matters which are crying for attention. This is not, of course, an occupational disease confined to music educators—it has infected all the humanities as well; and until the academic humanities can recapture a vital relationship with the contemporary, they will continue to demonstrate inadequacies similar to those so easily found in the plans of this Symposium. The Symposium was a profitable experience if only because it has indicated how careful we must all be to avoid spreading, in Professor Wind's words, that "really fatal disease, a kind of schizophrenia, in which the intellect ignores what the imagination pictures, and the imagination disregards what the intellect knows; both functions helplessly coexisting in a distracted mind."

RICHARD F. FRENCH

CONTENTS

MUSIC AND CRITICISM

INTRODUCTORY REMARKS

Archibald T. Davison

THE Music Department of Harvard University takes very great pleasure in welcoming you here in Sanders Theatre at the opening meeting of this three-day Symposium on Music Criticism. From the day on which the project was first put forward the Department has recognized the experimental and even the adventurous nature of this undertaking. Would there be, first of all, sufficient interest either public or professional to justify the thought and effort which must be expended on the planning and the manifold arrangements made necessary by an enterprise of this extent? The answer to that query was quickly and even clamorously given. The response has been widespread and numerically imposing. Frankly, we are astonished; and our bewildered gratification is surpassed only by our regret that owing to lack of space many requests for admission have had, perforce, to be denied.

We are a small department, relatively, and as I said a moment ago, this undertaking represented for us an adventure; one not unmixed with doubt. There were some, for example, who were apprehensive lest the addresses stimulate no more than polite discussion; they feared that there would be absent from the social meetings that ardor and intensity of dialectic which might, in the end, help to clarify important issues. I was never, I may say, of that party. Having a personal acquaintance with at least some of the speakers, and being aware of their capacity for provocative thought and language, I could anticipate no pallid reactions to whatever they might say. Indeed, it would not surprise me if in time to come these occasions, which, with proper academic reticence, we have entitled "Symposium on Music Criticism," came to be known as "The Three-Days War." Happily, it is my sole function to load the opening gun and thereafter to declare my unalterable neutrality and go immediately underground.

Upon one point, at least, the Department was in solid agreement: that regardless of the outcome, be it peace or be it war, someone ought to do something about music criticism; and I take it that in these three days we shall see an effort to submit its content to analysis, to establish its relation to other fields of criticism, and to reduce its objectives to some form of definition. That is what we hope for.

As far as I know, there are no statistics to show what proportion of the reading public concerns itself with music criticism; but if one may judge by the amount of space allotted to it in many newspapers—and for most persons music criticism means the writings on music in the daily press—then it is, I may say, no considerable rival of any other journalistic offering of which I have knowledge. This is certainly worthy of comment in view of the really astonishing amount of music of every type, which, whether we will or no, bids us give it attention. The radio and the phonograph, in particular, have in these last years incalculably increased the impact of music on the popular consciousness. For many music has become, with comparative suddenness, a source of great interest and stimulation; for others it is no more than an incitement to louder conversation; and for still others it has become a persistent and a violent abrasive. A picture you need not regard; a book you are not obliged to read; but from music in this year of our Lord in the United States of America there is no refuge. In the home, in the church, in the restaurant, in places of amusement, streaming from the windows of our neighbor's apartment, shrilling from the car parked in front of our house, that which sometimes rationally, and sometimes for lack of a properly characterizing epithet, we describe as music is a near-constant in our lives. To it we wake in the morning and we fall asleep at night; to it we are married and we are buried; and I doubt not that some day a medical generation will make it unanimous by decreeing that to it we shall be born.

In view of this, an enlightened musical laity is certainly desirable, but enlightenment presupposes some powers of discrimination; and it is by no means fanciful to speculate whether the sheer bulk of undistinguished and even negligible music which day after day pours forth on the air will not eventually drug us into an acceptance of all music at the level of the commonplace. If, in the future, the music critic is to command not the relatively restricted group which now reads his words, but a large and representative audience capable of understanding what he is talking about and of agreeing or disagreeing intelligently with him, then the critic must concern himself with the issue of musical taste as it exists in this country today. Many years ago President Eliot, in a pamphlet recommending needed changes in secondary education, declared music to be an essential in the life of every person who means to be—and these are his words—"cultivated, efficient and rationally happy." If there is virtue in an effort to make generally available an imperishable resource of life; if it is really desirable that we should one day see a generation which will listen understandingly to music, which will love it for its own sake and which will have a reasonable interest in competent and knowledgeable writing about it, then it may be said that the music critic is in a most favorable position to advance that cause by raising his voice loudly and insistently in behalf of a better world in the wilderness that is music education in the public schools of America.

And now, at the risk of tiresome repetition, may I say just once more, and finally, that we are entirely aware of the adventurous and possibly inconclusive nature of this undertaking. Perhaps nothing productive will emerge from these meetings. Perhaps the Music Department will, in the end, find itself criticized for attempting the impossible and for further beclouding an already nebulous issue. I can only say, however, that we entertain the most earnest hope that the addresses to come, and the discussion which must inevitably follow on them, will yield measurable, widespread, practical, and salutary results.

THE *RAISON D'ÊTRE* OF CRITICISM IN THE ARTS

E. M. Forster

BELIEVING as I do that music is the deepest of the arts and deep beneath the arts, I feel profoundly honored at being invited to speak at this Symposium. I have no standing. I am an amateur whose inadequacy will become all too obvious as he proceeds. Perhaps, though, you will remember in your charity that the word amateur implies love. I love music. Just to love it, or just to love anything or anybody is not enough. Love has to be clarified and controlled to give full value, and here is where criticism may help. But one has to start with love, one has, in the case of music, to want to hear the notes. If one has no initial desire to listen and no sympathy after listening, the notes will signify nothing, sound and fury, whatever their intellectual content.

My instructions are to discuss the *raison d'être* of criticism, and I have been asked to extend my references to the fine arts generally, and thus to attempt a broad introduction to the more specific and therefore more valuable contributions which will follow. It is a formidable assignment, and I feel the more anxious since the case against criticism is alarmingly strong, and much of my paper is bound to be a brief drawn up by the Devil's Advocate. I will postpone the evil day, and begin by indicating the case for criticism.

We are convened, I think, because we agree that previous training is desirable before we approach the arts. We mistrust untrained appreciation, believing that it often defeats its own ends. Appreciation ought to be enough. But unless we learn, by example and by failure and by comparison, appreciation will not bite. We shall tend to slip about on the surface of masterpieces, exclaiming with joy, but never penetrating. "Oh I do like Bach," cries one appreciator, and the other cries "Do you? I don't. I like Chopin." Exit in opposite directions chanting Bach and Chopin respectively, and hearing less the composers than their own voices. They resemble investors who proclaim the soundness of their financial investments. The Bach shares must not fall, the Chopin not fall further or one would have been proved a fool on the aesthetic stock exchange. The objection to untrained appreciation is not its naïveté but its tendency to lead to the appreciation of no one but oneself. Against such fatuity the critical spirit is a valuable corrective. Except at the actual moment of contact—and I shall have much to say on the subject of that moment—it is desirable to know why we like a work, and to be able to defend our preferences by argument. Our judgment has been strengthened and, if all goes well, the contacts will be intensified and increased and become more valuable. That is our hope in meeting here.

I add the proviso "if all goes well" because success lies on the knees of an unknown God. There is always the contrary danger: the danger that training may sterilize the sensitiveness that is being trained, that education may lead to knowledge instead of wisdom, and criticism to nothing but criticism; that spontaneous enjoyment like the Progress of Poesy in Matthew Arnold's poem may be checked because too much care has been taken to direct it into the right channel. Still it is a risk to be faced, and if no care had been taken the stream might have vanished even sooner. We hope criticism will help. We have faith in it as a respectable human activity, as an item in the larger heritage which differentiates us from the beasts.

How best can this activity be employed? One must allow it to construct aesthetic theories, though to the irreverent eyes of some of us they appear as traveling laboratories, beds of Procrustes whereon Milton is too long and Keats too short. In an age which is respectful to theory—as, for instance, the seventeenth century was respectful to Aristotle's theory of the dramatic unities —a theory may be helpful and stimulating, particularly to the sense of form. French tragedy could culminate in Racine because certain leading strings had been so willingly accepted that they were scarely felt. Corneille and Tasso were less happy. Corneille, having produced "The Cid," wasted much time trying to justify its deviations from Aristotle's rules, and Tasso wasted even more, for he published his theory of Christian epic poetry before he wrote the *Gerusalemme Liberata* which was to illustrate it. This epic was attacked by the critics because it deviated from what Aristotle said and also from what Tasso thought he might have said. Tasso was upset, became involved in three volumes of controversy, tried to write a second epic which should not deviate, failed, and went mad. Except perhaps in Russia, where the deviations of Shostakovich invite a parallel, in the modern world a theory has little power over the fine arts, for good or evil. We have no atmosphere where it can flourish, and the attempts of certain governments to generate such an atmosphere in bureaus are unlikely to succeed. The construction of aesthetic theories and their comparison is a desirable cultural exercise: the theories themselves are unlikely to spread far or to hinder or help.

A more practical activity for criticism is the sensitive dissection of particular works of art. What did the artist hope to do? What means did he employ, subconscious or conscious? Did he succeed, and if his success was partial, where did he fail? In such a dissection the tools should break as soon as they encounter any living tissue. The apparatus is nothing, the specimen all. Whether the forthcoming speakers at this Symposium will agree with so extreme a statement is doubtful, but we are promised particular examinations and I look forward to following these so far as an amateur can. It is delightful and profitable to enter into technicalities to the limit of one's poor ability, to continue as far as one can in the wake of an expert mind, to pursue an argument till it passes out of one's grasp. And to have, while this is going on, a particular work of art before one will be a great help. Besides learning about the work one increases one's powers. Criticism's central job seems to be education through precision.

A third activity, less important, remains to be listed, and since it lies more within my sphere than precision, I will discuss it at greater length. Criticism can stimulate. Few of us are sufficiently awake to the beauty and wonder of the world, and when art intervenes to reveal them, it sometimes acts in reverse and lowers a veil instead of raising it. This deadening effect can often be dispersed by a well-chosen word. We can be awakened by a remark which need not be profound or even true, and can be sent scurrying after the beauties and wonders we were ignoring. Journalism and broadcasting have their big opportunity here. Unsuited for synthesis or analysis, they can send out the winged word that carries us off to examine the original.

There is indeed a type of criticism which has no interpretative value, yet it should not be condemned. Much has been written about music, for instance, which has nothing to do with music and must make musicians smile. It usually describes the state into which the hearer was thrown as he sat on his chair at the concert and the visual images which occur to him in that sedentary position. Here is an example, and a very lovely one, from Walt Whitman. Whitman has heard one of Beethoven's master septets performed at Philadelphia (there is only

one Beethoven septet, but this the old boy did not know),
and the rendering of it on a small band of well-chosen
and perfectly combined instruments carried him away.

*Dainty abandon, sometimes as if Nature laughing on a
hillside in the sunshine; serious and firm monotonies, as
of winds; a horn sounding through the tangle of the
forest, and the dying echoes; soothing floating of waves,
but presently rising in surges, angrily lashing, muttering,
heavy; piercing peals of laughter, for interstices; now and
then weird, as Nature herself is in certain moods—but
mainly spontaneous, easy, careless—often the sentiment
of the postures of naked children playing or sleeping. It
did me good even to watch the violinists drawing their
bows so masterly—every motion a study. I allow'd myself, as I sometimes do, to wander out of myself. The
conceit came to me of a copious grove of singing birds,
and in their midst a simple harmonic duo, two human
souls, steadily asserting their own pensiveness, joyous-
ness.*

Here is adorable literature, but what has it to do with
Opus 20? A poet's imagination has been kindled. He
has allowed himself to wander out of himself, but not
into Beethoven's self, his presumable goal. He has evoked
the visual images congenial to him, and though in the
closing phrase there is a concert, it is not the one he
attended, for it took place in his Garden of Eden.

Another example of such criticism is to be found in
Proust. Proust is what Walt Whitman is not—sophisti-

cated, *soigné, rusé, maladif*. But he too listens to a septet and reacts to it visually, he is carried off his seat into a region which has nothing to do with the concert. It is the septet of Vinteuil, whom we have hitherto known as the composer of a violin sonata. Vinteuil himself, an obscure and unhappy provincial organist, has scarcely appeared, but his sonata, and particularly a phrase in it, *la petite phrase*, has been an actor in the long-drawn inaction of the novel. Character after character has listened to it, and has felt hope, jealousy, despair, peace, according to the circumstances into which *la petite phrase* has entered. We do not know what it sounds like, but its arrival always means emotional heightening.

Toward the end of the novel, the hero goes to a musical reception in Paris where a new work is to be performed. He does not bother to look at the program, being occupied with social trifles. It is a septet —the opening bars as somber, glacial, as if dawn had not yet risen over the sea. He finds himself in an unknown world where he understands nothing. Suddenly, into this bewilderment there falls—*la petite phrase*, a reference to the sonata. He is listening to a posthumous work of Vinteuil, of whose existence he was unaware. Everything falls into shape. It is as if he has walked in an unknown region and come across the little gate which belongs to the garden of a friend. The septet expands its immensities, now comprehensible. The dawn rises crimson out of the sea, hark midday rejoicings, give way to new images, and the little phrase of the sonata, once virginal and shy, is august, quivering with colors, finally matured.

Now, these visual wanderings are not entirely to my taste, not perhaps to yours. Whitman's has its own naïve merit, but in the case of Proust, who is pretentious culturally, we feel uneasy. Shall we then say that they do not and cannot help us musically at all? I think this is too severe. The septets of Beethoven and of Vinteuil have come no nearer to us, but we have been excited, we have been disposed to listen to sounds, we have been challenged to test the descriptions and to decide whether we agree with them. This general sharpening of interest is desirable. It can be effected in various ways; by a legitimate critic like Donald Tovey, by a grand old boy at Philadelphia, or by a snobby Frenchman in the Faubourg St. Germain. All ways are not equally good. Those who hear music will always interpret it best. But those who don't hear it after the first few notes have also their use. Their wanderings, their visual images, their dreams, help to sharpen us. They recall us to the importance of sounds, and, their inferiors in other ways, we may perhaps manage to listen to the sounds longer than they did.

Examples of higher musical value are to be found in the early journalism of Bernard Shaw. Though Shaw is a man of letters, like Whitman and Proust, and readily runs after his own thoughts and pictorial images, he does manage to remember the music. He can interpret as well as stimulate. He can say, for instance, of Haydn:

"Haydn would have been among the greatest had he been driven to that terrible eminence; but we are fortunate enough in having had at least one man of genius who was happy enough in the Valley of Humiliation to feel no compulsion to struggle on through the Valley of the Shadow of Death." What a sensitive and just reflection! How admirably it expresses that turning away from the tragic so often displayed by Haydn—for instance in the opening of the C Major Symphony, Opus 97—turning away not because he is afraid of tragedy, which would discomfort the listener, but because he prefers not to be tragic. This is an eccentricity in Haydn, and, apprehending it, Shaw convinces us that he is inside music and could have criticized it more deeply, had his career and his inclinations allowed.

I like, in this connection, jokes about music, irresponsible folly which sometimes kicks a door open as it flies. They, too, may incline us to listen to sounds. When the English humorist, Beachcomber says, "Wagner is the Puccini of music," he means rather more than he says. Besides guying a well-worn formula, he pierces Grand Opera itself, and reveals Brünnehilde and Butterfly transfixed on the same mischievous pin. I like, too, the remark of an uncle of mine, a huntin', fishin', and shootin', sportin' sort of uncle, whose aversion to the arts was very genuine. "They tell me," he said one day thoughtfully, "they tell me Music's like a gun, it hurts less when you let it off yourself." Besides getting in a well-directed gibe, and discomposing my aunt who adored Mendelssohn, he indicated very neatly the gulf between artist on the one hand and the critic on the other. Those who are involved and those who appraise are never hurt in the same way. This is, as a matter of fact, going to be our chief problem here, and perhaps it will come the fresher because my uncle hit at it in his slapdash fashion before striding back to his dogs.

For now our trouble starts. We can readily agree that criticism has educational and cultural value, that it helps to civilize the community, builds up standards, forms theories, stimulates, directs, encourages the individual to enjoy the world into which he has been born; and, on its destructive side, it exposes fraud and pretentiousness and checks conceit. These are substantial achievements. But I would like if I could to establish its *raison d'être* on a higher basis than that of public utility. I would like to discover some spiritual parity between it and the objects it criticizes, and this is going to be difficult. The difficulty has been variously expressed. One writer, Mr. F. L. Lucas, has called criticism a charming parasite; another, Chekhov, complains it is a gadfly which hinders the oxen from ploughing; a third, Lord Kames, compares it to an imp which distracts critics from their objective and incites them to criticize each other. My own trouble is not so much that it is a parasite, a gadfly, or an imp, but that there is a basic difference between the critical and creative state of mind, and to the consideration of that difference I would now invite your attention.

What about the creative state? In it a man is taken out of himself. He lets down, as it were, a bucket into his subconscious, and draws up something which is normally beyond his reach. He mixes this thing with his normal experiences, and out of the mixture he makes a work of art. It may be a good work of art or a bad one—we are not here examining the question of quality—but whether it is good or bad it will have been compounded in this unusual way, and he will wonder afterwards how he did it. Such seems to be the creative process. It may employ much technical ingenuity and worldly knowledge, it may profit by critical standards, but mixed up with it is this stuff from the bucket, this subconscious stuff, which is not procurable on demand. And when the process is over, when the picture or symphony or lyric or novel (or whatever it is) is complete, the artist, looking back on it, will wonder how on earth he did it. And indeed, he did not do it on earth.

A perfect example of the creative process is to be found in *Kubla Khan*. Assisted by opium, Coleridge had his famous dream, and dipped deep into the subconscious. Waking up, he started to transcribe it, and was proceeding successfully when that person from Porlock unfortunately called on business.

> *Weave a circle round him thrice*
> *And close your eyes with holy dread*
> *For he on honeydew hath fed*
> *And drunk the milk of Paradise—*

and in came the person from Porlock. Coleridge could not resume. His connection with the subconscious had snapped. He had created and did not know how he had done it. As Professor Livingston Lowes has shown, many fragments of Coleridge's day-to-day reading are embedded in *Kubla Khan*, but the poem itself belongs to another world, which he was seldom to record.

The creative state of mind is akin to a dream. In Coleridge's case it was a dream. In other cases—Jane Austen's, for instance—the dream is remote or sedate. But even Jane Austen, looking back upon *Emma*, could have thought "Dear me, how came I to write that? It is not ill-contrived." There is always, even with the most realistic artist, the sense of withdrawal from his own creation, the sense of surprise.

The French writer, Paul Claudel, gives the best description known to me of the creative state. It occurs in his poem, "La Ville." A poet is speaking. He has been asked whence his inspiration comes, and how it is that when he speaks everything becomes explicable although he explains nothing. He replies:

I do not speak what I wish, but I conceive in sleep,
And I cannot explain whence I draw my breath, for it
   is my breath which is drawn out of me.
I expand the emptiness within me, I open my mouth, I
   breathe in the air, I breathe it out.
I restore it in the form of an intelligible word,
And having spoken I know what I have said.

There is a further idea in the passage, which my brief English paraphrase has not attempted to convey: the idea that if the breathing in is *in*spiration the breathing out is *ex*spiration, a prefiguring of death, when the life of a man will be drawn out of him by the unknown force for the last time. Creation and death are closely connected for Claudel. I'm confining myself, though, to his description of the creative act, and ask you to observe how precisely it describes what happened in *Kubla Khan*. There is conception in sleep, there is the connection between the subconscious and the conscious, which has to be effected before the work of art can be born, and there is the surprise of the creator at his own creation.

> *Je restitue une parole intelligible,*
> *Et l'ayant dite, je sais ce que j'ai dit.*

Which is exactly what happened to Coleridge. He knew what he had said, but as soon as inspiration was interrupted he could not say any more.

After this glance at the creative state, let us glance at the critical. The critical state has many merits, and employs some of the highest and subtlest faculties of man. But it is grotesquely remote from the state responsible for the works it affects to expound. It does not let down buckets into the subconscious. It does not conceive in sleep, or know what it has said after it has said it. Think before you speak is criticism's motto; speak before you think creation's. Nor is criticism discon-

certed by people arriving from Porlock, in fact it sometimes comes from Porlock itself. While not excluding
imagination and sympathy, it keeps them and all the
faculties under control, and only employs them when
they promise to be helpful.

Thus equipped, it advances on its object. It has two
aims. The first and the more important is aesthetic. It
considers the object in itself, as an entity, and tells us
what it can about its life. The second aim is subsidiary:
the relation of the object to the rest of the world. Problems of less relevance are considered, such as the conditions under which the work of art was composed, the
influences which formed it (criticism adores influences),
the influence it has exercised on subsequent works, the
artist's life, the lives of the artist's father and mother,
prenatal possibilities, and so on, straying this way into
psychology and that way into history. Much of the
above is valuable, but what meanwhile has become of
Monteverdi's Vespers, or the Great Mosque at Delhi,
or the *Frogs* of Aristophanes, or any other work which
you happen to have in mind? I throw these three objects
at you because they happen to be in my own mind as I
write. I have been hearing the Vespers, seeing the *Frogs*,
and thinking about the Delhi Mosque. If we wheel up
an aesthetic theory—the best attainable, and there are
some excellent ones—if we wheel it up and apply it with
its measuring rods and pliers and forceps, its calipers
and catheters to Vespers, Mosque, and *Frogs*, we are
visited at once by a sense of the grotesque. It doesn't

work, two universes have not even collided, they have been juxtaposed. There is no spiritual parity. And if criticism strays from her central aesthetic quest to influences and psychological and historical considerations, something does happen then, contact is established. But no longer with a work of art.

A work of art is a curious object. Isn't it infectious? Unlike machinery, hasn't it the power of transforming the person who encounters it toward the condition of the person who created it? (I use the clumsy phrase "towards the condition" on purpose.) We—we, the beholders, or listeners, or whatever we are—undergo a change analogous to creation. We are rapt into a region near to that where the artist worked, and like him when we return to earth we feel surprised. To claim we actually entered his state and became cocreators with him there is presumptuous. However much excited I am by Brahms' Fourth Symphony I cannot suppose I feel Brahms' excitement, and probably what he felt is not what I understand as excitement. But there has been an infection from Brahms through his music to myself. Something has passed. I have been transformed toward his condition, he has called me out of myself, he has thrown me into a subsidiary dream; and when the passacaglia is trodden out, and the transformation closed, I too feel surprise.

Unfortunately, this infection, this sense of coöperation with a creator—which is the supremely important step in our pilgrimage through the fine arts—is the one step over which criticism cannot help. She can prepare us for it generally, and educate us to keep our senses open, but she has to withdraw when reality approaches, like Virgil from Dante on the summit of Purgatory. With the coming of love, we have to rely on Beatrice, whom we have loved all along, and if we have never loved Beatrice we are lost. We shall remain pottering about with theories and influences and psychological and historical considerations—supports useful in their time, but they must be left behind at the entry of Heaven. I would not suggest that our comprehension of the fine arts is or should be of a nature of a mystic union. But, as in mysticism, we enter an unusual state, and we can only enter it through love. Putting it more prosaically, we cannot understand music unless we desire to hear it. And so we return to the earth.

Let us reconsider that troublesome object, the work of art, and observe another way in which it is recalcitrant to criticism. I am thinking of its freshness. So far as it is authentic, it presents itself as eternally virgin. It expects always to be heard or read or seen for the first time, always to cause surprise. It does not expect to be studied, still less does it present itself as a crossword puzzle, only to be solved after much reëxamination. If it does that, if it parades a mystifying element, it is, to that extent, not a work of art, not an immortal Muse but a Sphinx who dies as soon as her riddles are answered. The work of art assumes the existence of the perfect listener or spectator, and is indifferent to the fact that no such person exists. It does not allow for our ignorance, and it does not call for our knowledge.

This eternal freshness in creation presents a difficulty to the critic, who when he hears or reads or sees a work a second time rightly profits by what he has heard or read or seen of it the first time, and studies and compares, remembers and analyses, and often has to reject his original impressions as trivial. He may thus in the end gain a just and true opinion of the work, but he ought to remain startled and this is usually beyond him. Take Beethoven's Ninth Symphony, the one in A. Isn't it in A? The opening bars announce the key as explicitly as fifths can, leaving us only in doubt as to whether the movement will decide on the major or minor mode. In the fifteenth bar comes the terrifying surprise, the pounce into D minor, which tethers the music, however far it wanders, right down to the ineluctable close. Can one hope to feel that terror and surprise twice? Can one avoid hearing the opening bars as a preparation for the pounce—and thus miss the life of the pounce? Can we combine experience and innocence? I think we can. The willing suspension of experience is possible, it is possible to become like a child who says "Oh!" each time the ball bounces, although he has seen it bounce before and knows it must bounce. It is possible but it is rare. The critic who is thoroughly versed in the score of the Ninth Symphony and can yet hear the opening bars as a trembling introduction in A to the unknown, has reached the highest rank in his profession. Most of us are content to remain well-informed. It is so restful to be well-informed. We forget that Beethoven intended his symphony to be heard always for the first time. We forget with still greater ease that Tchaikovsky intended the same for his Piano Concerto in B flat minor. Dubious for good reasons of that thumping affair, we sometimes scold it for being "stale"—a ridiculous accusation, for it, too, was created as an eternal virgin; it, too, should startle each time it galumphs down the waltz. No doubt the concerto, and much music, has been too often performed, just as some pictures have been too often looked at. Freshness of reception is exhausted more rapidly by a small or imperfect object than by a great one. Nevertheless, the objects themselves are eternally new, it is the recipient who may wither. You remember how at the opening of Goethe's *Faust*, Mephistopheles, being stale himself, found the world stale, and reported it as such to the Almighty. The archangels took no notice of him and continued to sing of eternal freshness.

The critic ought to combine Mephistopheles with the Archangels, experience with innocence. He ought to know everything inside out, and yet be surprised. Virginia Woolf—who was both a creative artist and a critic—believed in reading a book twice. The first time she abandoned herself to the author unreservedly. The second time she treated him with severity and allowed him to get away with nothing which he could not justify. After these two readings she felt qualified to discuss the book. Hers is good rule-of-thumb advice. But it does not take us to the heart of the problem, which is super-rational. For we ought really to read the book in two ways at once, and to listen to music similarly. We ought to perform a miracle the nature of which was hinted at by the Almighty when he said he was always glad to receive Mephistopheles in Heaven and hear him chat.

I speak tentatively in the presence of this expert audience, but it seems to me that we are most likely to perform that miracle in the case of music. Music, more than the other arts, postulates a double existence. It exists in time, takes half an hour to play or whatever it is, and also exists outside time, instantaneously. With no philosophic training, I cannot put my belief clearly, but I can conceive myself hearing a piece as it goes by and also when it has finished. In the latter case I should hear it as an entity, as a piece of sound-architecture, not as a sound-sequence, not as something divisible into bars. Yet it would be organically connected with the concert-hall performance. Architecture and sequence would, in my apprehension, be more closely fused than the two separate readings of a book in Virginia Woolf's.

The claim of criticism to take us to the heart of the Arts must therefore be disallowed. Another claim has been made for it, a more precise one. It has been suggested that criticism can help an artist to improve his work. If that be true, a *raison d'être* is established at once. Criticism becomes an important figure, a handmaid to beauty, holding out the sacred lamp in whose light creation proceeds, feeding the lamp with oil, trimming the wick when it flares or smokes. There must be many artists, musicians and others, in this audience, and it would be interesting to know whether criticism has helped them in their work, and if so how. Has she held up the lamp? No doubt she illuminates past mistakes or merits, that certainly is within her power, but has the better knowledge of them any practical value?

A remark of the poet, Mr. C. Day Lewis, is interesting in this connection. It comes at the opening of his admirable new book, *The Poetic Image*. He says:

There is something formidable for the poet in the idea of criticism—something, dare I say it?—almost unreal. He writes a poem, then he moves on to the new experience, the next poem: and when a critic comes along and tells him what is right or wrong about the first poem, he has a feeling of irrelevance.

Something almost unreal. That is a just remark. The poet is always developing and moving on, and when his creative state is broken into by comments on something he has put behind him, he feels bewildered. His reaction is "What are you talking about? Must you?" Once again, and in its purest form, the division between the critical and creative states, the absence of spiritual parity, becomes manifest. In its purest form because poetry is an extreme form of art, and is a convenient field for experiment. My own art, the mixed art of fiction, is less suitable, yet I can truly say with Mr. Day Lewis that I have nearly always found criticism irrelevant. When

I am praised, I am pleased; when I am blamed, I am displeased; when I am told I am elusive, I am surprised —but neither the pleasure nor the sorrow nor the astonishment makes any difference when next I enter the creative state. One can eliminate a particular defect perhaps; to substitute merit is the difficulty. I remember that in one of my earlier novels I was blamed for the number of sudden deaths in it which were said to amount to forty-four per cent of the fictional population. I took heed and arranged that characters in subsequent novels should die less frequently and give previous notice where possible by means of illness or some other acceptable device. But I was not inspired to put anything vital in the place of sudden deaths. The only remedy for a defect is inspiration, the subconscious stuff that comes up in the bucket. A piece of contemporary music, to my ear, has a good many sudden deaths in it; the phrases expire as rapidly as the characters in my novel, the chords cut each other's throats, the arpeggio has a heart attack, the fugue gets into a nose dive. But these defects —if defects they be—are doubtless vital to the general conception. They are not to be remedied by substituting sweetness. And the musicians would do well to ignore the critic even when they admit the justice of the particular criticism.

Only in two ways can criticism help the artist a little with his work. The first is general. He ought—if he keeps company at all—to keep good company. To be alone may be best—to be alone was what Fate reserved for Beethoven. But if he wishes to consort with ideas and standards and the works of his fellow—and he usually has to in the modern world—he must beware of the second rate. It means a relaxation of fiber, a temptation to rest on his own superiority. I do not desire to use the words "superior" and "inferior" about human individuals; in an individual so many factors are present that one cannot grade him. But one can legitimately apply them to cultural standards, and the artist should be critical here and alive in particular to the risks of the clique. The clique is a valuable social device, which only a fanatic would condemn; it can protect and encourage the artist. It is the artist's duty, if he wants to be in a clique, to choose a good one, and to take care it doesn't make him bumptious, sterile or silly. The lowering of critical standards in what one may call daily studio life, their corruption by adulation or jealousy, may lead to inferior work. Good standards may lead to good work. That is all that there seems to be to say about this vague assistance, and maybe it was not worth saying.

The second way in which criticism can help the artist is more specific. It can help him over details, niggling details, minutiae of style. To refer to my own work again, I have certainly benefited by being advised not to use the word "but" so often. I have had a university education, you see, and it disposes one to overwork that particular conjunction. It is the strength of the academic mind to be fair and see both sides of a question.

It is its weakness to be timid and to suffer from that fear-of-giving-oneself-away disease of which Samuel Butler speaks. Both its strength and its weakness incline it to the immoderate use of "but." You have heard a good many "buts" in this paper, but not as many as if I hadn't been warned. The writer of the opposed type, the extrovert, the man who knows what he knows, and likes what he likes, and doesn't care who knows it—he should be subject to the opposite discipline. He should be criticized because he never uses "but"; he should be tempted to employ the qualifying clause. The man who has a legal mind should probably go easy on his "ifs." Fiddling little matters. Yes, I know. The sort of trifling help which criticism can give the artist. She cannot help him in great matters.

With these random considerations my paper must close. The latter part of it has been overshadowed and perhaps obsessed by my consciousness of the gulf between the creative and critical states. Perhaps the gulf does not exist; perhaps it does not signify; perhaps I have been making a gulf out of a molehill. But in my view it does prevent the establishment of a first class *raison d'être* for criticism in the arts. The only activity which can establish such a *raison d'être* is love. However cautiously, with whatever reservations, after whatsoever purifications, we must come back to love. That alone raises us to the coöperation with the artist which is the sole reason for our aesthetic pilgrimage. That alone promises spiritual parity. My main conclusion on criticism has, therefore, to be unfavorable, nor have I succeeded in finding that it has given substantial help to artists.

The earlier part of the paper was confined to subsidiary topics, and here a defence for criticism can easily be established. Criticism can educate, theorise, analyse, stimulate—admirable achievements. And when I say that defence is easy, I do not mean that I performed it adequately. Much more could have been said, and what was said could have been much better said. It has been a pleasure as well as an anxiety to prepare this paper. Most of it has been written in my own Cambridge, and while it was in progress I received the kindest and most encouraging letters from your Cambridge. They stimulated me to complete a task which is really beyond me. For I am not a musician, I am not even a critic, and it does seem somewhat daring to fly the Atlantic and address people who are both.

THE SCOPE OF MUSIC CRITICISM

Roger Sessions

IN PREPARING this paper I have been reminded of a luncheon which I attended some twenty years ago, at the Tavern Club in Boston. The guest of honor and speaker of the occasion was Mr. Ernest Newman, the well-known English music critic. His remarks were devoted to the thesis that it is more difficult to criticize a piece of music than to compose it. It was a serious discussion; and I regret to say I do not remember his arguments. But I remember very well my momentary indignation at what seemed to me a professional slight, an implied belittling of the work of the composer.

On more mature thought, however, I felt less and less inclined to quarrel with Mr. Newman, or at least with this particular thesis. The question of relative difficulty is of course eminently irrelevant as well as quite incalculable; and one may also very well recall the saying which I have heard ascribed to Victor Hugo who when asked if it were difficult to write an epic poem is said to have replied, "Madame, it is either easy or impossible." The same saying may perhaps in the deepest sense be applied to all works of art. The composer, for instance, may well encounter difficult problems of execution, even quite aside from the question of his mastery of his technique—which, after all, is expected of him. But if he finds the conception difficult—if he is ever in real doubt as to what he wants, his plight is a very serious one. His conception may either develop slowly, or be with him in essence from the start—most artists have, I fancy, had both experiences; but if it ever assumes the aspect, for him, of a problem to be solved, his work is in that measure almost surely predestined to failure. With the embodiment of his conception, his work is finished, and the success of a later revision of his work will depend precisely on the extent to which he is able to recapture both his conception and his relationship to it.

With the critic it is perhaps different; his work is never finished and, exactly when it is most worth while—when the objects of his criticism are works or questions in which he is most passionately interested—it will consist in a constant process of revision which, at best, will go on in other hands even after the critic himself has disappeared. His work is, indeed, by its very nature problematical and inconclusive; and though he doubtless strives for finality, he can achieve it only in relation to works which have lost their vitality, and in regard to which criticism has become irrelevant.

In all this I have of course been exaggerating differences and ignoring similarities. In a subtler and deeper sense the composer's work, too, is a continuous effort —his inner development reflects the development of his personality and his experience as surely as do the critic's; just as the critic's successive judgments even of the same work may well have their independent value. Both however have a still deeper bond in common: that both, when they are contemporaries, are in a very real and inescapable sense products of a common cultural situation and, in however varying manners, parts of a whole.

This is of course obvious enough; but I think it is worth emphasizing here. When we speak of "contemporary music" we are generally referring to the work of contemporary composers and more specifically to that part of it which differentiates itself most sharply from the work of previous generations, and in particular of the generation immediately preceding. I think it is not often enough pointed out that the musical spirit of any given period is exemplified not only in the work of its composers, but also in the prevailing modes of interpretation and the prevailing tastes. It is very easy, for example, to note the wide differences between the tastes and the interpretative modes of today and those of thirty-five years ago, and it is no way fantastic to discover that these differences in aesthetic attitude find quite exact parallels in the differences between the actual creative productions of the two periods. Our contemporary emphasis on the punctilious following of the composer's directions in the interpretation of, say, the Beethoven Symphonies; the revival of half or even wholly forgotten symphonies of Haydn; the resurgence of Verdi and Berlioz; the relative eclipse of Liszt—all these are a few symptoms of a changed musical attitude, of which other and more striking symptoms are to be found in the music of Bartók and Stravinsky and Hindemith.

I emphasize this point because I believe very strongly that the critic's primary function and his deepest obligation are to be found in his relationship to the musical community of which he is a part, and his recognition, first of all, of the fact that he is inescapably a part of it. I call to mind the remark which I read some years ago in one of our more important organs of musical comment, to the effect that while the level of creative work in the United States was vastly lower than that of Europe, the level of criticism was by so much higher. The observation seemed to me naïve and meaningless precisely because it implied a detachment of the critic from the primary object of his criticism. It seemed to me an implied admission of the justice of an estimate of American musical affairs which I had so often heard voiced abroad—that American musical achievement consisted in an overwhelming measure of the ability to pay for what were, in their relationship to our scene, essentially luxury products from Europe. The observation seemed also to relegate musical criticism to the status of an appraisal of these goods in relation to their value in the luxury market; for if a living culture, as I believe, consists primarily in the production and not merely the consumption of cultural goods, and consequently of values, the experience and the work of the composer stands at its very center, and the critic finds his point of departure in the common musical experience which is at its most intense in the most important productions of its composers.

If this be true, the critic is essentially the composer's collaborator. I do not of course mean that his judgment must be always favorable, or indeed, necessarily ever wholly so, either toward the artists who are his contemporaries or to the so-called "tendencies" which they represent; but that his first and most serious objective should be the understanding of his own musical time and place, and that without this understanding of what is most immediate he almost certainly lacks a vital portion of that which is necessary to a living relationship with the products of other times and places. His contacts are likely to be secondary contacts, his knowledge book-knowledge rather than that primarily derived from experience.

I would therefore ask of the critic, first, an understanding and conscientious judgment of his own musical time and place, the time and place of which he is unavoidably but one part and one voice. Of what elements should this judgment consist, and how is he to arrive at it?

It is scarcely original to point out that we live in a period in which our intellectual life is dominated by science, and that our habits of thought tend to approach the methods of the sciences. In criticism of the arts a familiar cry is for "objectivity," and an overwhelmingly prevalent tendency is the search for objective criteria. Thus music is held up for measurement to any number of frames of reference—aesthetic or technical systems, national "styles," and even political ideologies. No doubt such frames of reference can have their value, but I would like to suggest that they are at best secondary, and at worst evasions of the first and far more difficult consideration, which is the inherent quality of the music itself. I would like to suggest first of all that there is no possibility whatever of an objective method of determining this issue. This inherent quality is precisely the quality in the music which must be felt and experienced; the capacity for feeling it is developed through experience and through that aptitude for musical experience which is generally called musical instinct. In order to distinguish the reality from the appearance of musical imagination or invention the attitude of the critic must be anything but "objective"; he must first of all be ready to enjoy the music or, if you prefer, to feel it and to receive its impact or its message. If he feels nothing, the music has not yet begun to exist for him—it has not yet begun to be music, but remains at best "style" or "tendency," generalized and without real identity. The same is essentially true if the music arouses his response through its associations, its context, the circumstances of its production or performance, or through any other means than the direct impact of its melodies, harmonies, sonorities, or rhythms. By experience the critic will have learned in one degree or another to evaluate his impressions in terms of their intensity, their directness, their coherence and their durability. He will know, for example, whether he is tempted to hear the work again, and to explore it further; if he is conscientious he will do so if the work gives him the smallest encouragement, since he will have learned that music is essentially designed not to be simply heard, but to be experienced to its fullest extent. He will perhaps have reflected that it is not primarily for listeners at all, but for performers, and especially singers, that the composer fashions his works, and that any musical work is understood only when it is inwardly reproduced—much as the reader of poetry grasps the rhythm and sound of a poem through reproducing them in his imagination.

The critic's primary concern, then, must be the work itself: whether it really possesses the quality of direct communication; whether the composer has really felt, or, as I would prefer to say—for the term seems to me simpler and less misleading—whether he has felt, or *inwardly heard*, something which he has been able to communicate—that is, to make his listener inwardly hear. He will know from many experiences that composers possess this quality in very varying degrees, and he will, if he is gifted and at the same time untroubled by preconceived ideas, have developed a more or less reliable power of discrimination between what is genuine and what is false. I stress a lack of preconceived idea precisely because strained efforts toward objectivity seem so often, through emphasis on so-called objective criteria, to produce a kind of sectarianism and a lack of receptivity. The true critic must be able to distinguish varying degrees of quality in types of music which are unsympathetic to him as well as in those which are sympathetic, and even to admit that a good work of an unsympathetic *tendency* is preferable to a bad one of sympathetic tendency—he is no true critic if he does not do this.

It is at this point that the creative artist often fails. This failure is not universal. Indeed, one of the wisest and most genuinely educated men I have known—a critic of one of the other arts—once said to me, "The creative artist is the best critic of all, provided he takes the trouble." The proviso is of course a very considerable one—he seldom takes the trouble, and in fact generally has no desire or incentive to do so. He is by his very nature absorbed in his own conceptions; sometimes, and especially in our own day, afraid to open himself to other influences lest they disturb his serenity, and sometimes jealous. The fact remains, however, that some of the greatest critics of the past have been creative artists whose generosity or whose vital curiosity have enabled them to bring their best powers to the task of criticism, and who could see their individual predilections or personal destinies at times in the perspective of their love for music as such. Far more frequently, no doubt, even the greatest composers have failed to make the effort which this type of criticism demands, and have remained poor or indifferent critics. It should be noted, however, that not composers alone, but professional critics as well, often become the victims of similar bias.

I have stressed this question of immediate and primary contact with music, not because I imagine that it is ever entirely absent from a critic's appraisal of a musical work, but rather because one hears it so seldom given as the reason for a critical judgment, while I believe it is in reality the primary one—the court of final appeal, to which others are necessarily subordinate. Technical questions, for example, have no meaning whatever except in relation to this primary contact. We speak so often, for example, of "craftsmanship"—so-called—in terms which relegate the mature composer to the same level as a first-class student. It is as idle to praise a composer for his craftsmanship as to praise an engineer because his bridge does not collapse. On any other basis, after all, technique becomes superfluous and even obtrusive; one may even say that it is not genuine technique unless it is quite inseparable from the musical content, and in fact identical with it. The value of Bach's *Die Kunst der Fuge* or such a contemporary work as Hindemith's *Ludus Tonalis* is neither enhanced nor diminished by the technical complexities which these works embody—these complexities belong to the essence, the conception, of the works, and would otherwise be meaningless and tasteless. Similarly, technical devices which do not come to life in the perceptible shape of the work must be considered as at best the purely private affair of the composer, introduced for his own purposes but irrelevant apart from his own psychology—not, in any case, relevant to either the character or the value of the work.

Similarly, technical flaws in a work—if they are genuine—are most often flaws not of execution but of conception. The composer's impulse has faltered, or his attention has wavered, his ideas have not been clear, or he has surrendered momentarily to convention. I am referring of course to the kind of flaws which arise in the center and under the sign of the composition itself, not to practical miscalculations, such as mistakes in instrumentation, or departures from conventional procedure such as Rimski-Korsakov found in *Boris Godunov*. But judgment based primarily on technical criticism I believe to be irrelevant unless the critic has the power to make clear the technical facts in terms of a faulty—that is to say, unrealized—conception, or, on the other hand, a successful one.

Having established his initial contact with the musical work, and gained in this way an essential insight into its nature, the critic is bound to fit it into larger patterns. He will inevitably judge it, for instance, according to his own aesthetic predilections. He will pass, in other words, from the phase of a critic of works to that of a critic of tendencies and of aesthetic aims. If I have stressed the necessity of the first phase, it is not because I wish in any sense to belittle the importance of this second one, but rather to make clear that no judgment of aesthetic tendency is possible except on the basis of a real understanding of, and insight into, what the composer communicates. For a vital aesthetic movement is embodied not in programs or intentions but in works, and can be appraised only in terms of those works. To take two examples from recent musical history: neoclassicism, or the twelve tone technique, are to be judged, not as such, but only in terms of their successful embodiment in more or less convincing works—they can prevail only as the works prevail, and then the victory will be for the works and not the systems and principles. Need one quote musical history in proof of this? Each generation is obliged to solve its problems afresh and a tendency or system can be nothing more than a point of departure.

The critic of tendencies must therefore beware of the easy criteria which systems afford. This, however, is not the whole story. For aesthetic tendencies are, insofar as they are vital, the embodiment of deeper attitudes—not so much strictly artistic attitudes as basically human ones; and a thoughtful critic will eventually find himself, perhaps, regarding them in that light. I am not referring to what is sometimes called "social significance," which is to an overwhelming extent a matter of association, not of the essence of the work itself. Thus, for good or ill, Beethoven's Eroica Symphony is loved to all appearances equally well by those who see in it a glorification of Napoleon, the standard-bearer of Revolutionary France, and by those who prefer to see in it the glorification of the head of the French state.

Thus I was told in Germany by a German radical that young and revolutionary minded people there were stirred by Stravinsky's *Symphonie de Psaumes*, regardless of its religious associations, because it constituted for them a new and exciting experience. We must therefore seek deeper than mere association if we are to arrive at the final questions which a critic will find himself asking—and to which he is least likely to find a satisfactory answer. Instead of "social significance" he will of course seek "significance," and he will try, perhaps never wholly successfully, to define it. But he may well find himself thinking not only of aesthetic creeds but of personalities and of works in terms of basic human attitudes. I hesitate to use the much-abused word "moral"; it suggests not only certain primitive misconceptions regarding the nature and function of art, but calls up visions of censorship and other highly dangerous practices. Yet I think we cannot possibly evade the fact that, for instance, those of us who find Wagner's music distasteful, do so not on the ground that he was in any sense an artist of secondary stature, which he certainly was not—not primarily because Wotan and Siegfried and Parsifal were unpleasant characters beloved by Hitler and his followers (we can ignore them by treating them as we do story-book characters who are often even more unpleasant)—but because the music, even apart from its dramatic associations, embodies basic human attitudes and gestures which we find in the last analysis repulsive: either because the passage of time has robbed them of a large part of their magic and made them seem stilted and mechanical, or because we see in them the grandiose and essentially cruel gestures of the magician whom Nietzsche described so well, and instinctively recoil from an art in which the aesthetic shudder or caress has become an end in itself, a tool in the hands of a supreme egoist whose art, so genuinely expressive at times, consisted so much of calculated effect at others.

I have given this one example, partly because it seems to me so obvious and so clear, in order to hint at the critic's ultimate and most difficult problem. For the question of the relation of art to society as a whole, however much we may dismiss some of the more naïve and more tendentious forms in which it is raised, has inevitably arisen in a period like our own in which vast changes are everywhere in progress, and in which even human survival has become problematical. In such a world the basic human attitudes become decisive, superficiality becomes an encumbrance, and in the last analysis intolerable, and the responsibility of not only artists and critics but of every thinking human being a decisive one.

I have tried to deal with what seems to me the essentials of musical criticism rather than with certain of its specific details—the question of performance and interpretation, for instance, the separate question of musical journalism and its relation to criticism as such, or the relation of the critic to the economic colossus which determines to such a great extent the course of our musical life today. I should like to close with the observation, once more, that the work of the critic is never complete, and his judgment never definitive. Any one who has observed, over a period of years, the changing musical climate, the rise and fall of reputations, the fluctuations of prevailing style and tendency, the shifting concepts of interpretation, and the varying reactions of critics to them, must come to realize that decisive judgments are made, not by critics or other individuals, but by numerous forces which frequently—even constantly—work in ways which are surprising to all concerned.

It is easy to be pessimistic about the fate of mankind, and I would be the last to minimize the dangers with which the human species is confronted. These dangers come, in fact, not from outside, but from within the heart and mind of man himself. The illness is a deep-seated one—chronic and possibly inherent in man's nature. The recovery of the patient is problematical and the danger both mortal and immediate.

These are of course near platitudes, and must form the greater part of the premises of every adult man today. It is not only culture or civilization that stands in imminent danger of destruction.

But assuming the survival of culture we must assume also that cultural values will survive, that genuine quality in art will always prevail in any moderately long-range view, and that the qualities which we value—richness of imagination and invention, intensity and lucidity of expression, the basic equilibrium which is the ultimate sign of both inner and outer mastery—will always in the end prevail, and that, with all fluctuations of critical climate, and whatever the destiny of the individual artist or aesthetic tendency or epoch, art itself will go on; and that whatever qualities are genuine will make their contribution, either directly or indirectly, to its growth and its survival. There is no more destructive belief in the world than pessimism in this regard, and no more dangerous symptom of mankind's various and complicated ills than the widespread and visible belief in propaganda, and tendency to rely on it, which such pessimism engenders. As a final word I would simply point out that for the musical critic in particular such pessimism is fatal. His undiminished love for music, his sensitiveness to tones and rhythms and harmonies, to timbres and sonorities, his fundamental responsiveness to music and his belief in its reality, are the very essence of his task and the condition of his validity.

THE CRITICAL NATURE OF A
WORK OF ART

Edgar Wind

WHEN I first heard of the title of this paper—"The Critical Nature of a Work of Art"—I had considerable misgivings, but these the organizers of the Symposium were kind enough to dispel. Perhaps my apprehensions should have revived when I listened to Mr. Forster's speech; for if his argument should prevail, the "critical nature of a work of art" would have to be dismissed as a contradiction in terms. But susceptible though I was to the enchantment of his demonstration, I confess I was emboldened by it rather than deterred: and so I shall begin this imprudent venture by assailing Mr. Forster's conclusions.

He has opened before us a forbidding gulf separating the creative artist from the critic, a chasm so vast that, in his view, it cannot be crossed except by love; and yet he left some of us with the impression that no love was ever lost between these two opponents. As he contrasted their respective roles, they seemed to face each other through a void produced by the absolute disparity of their methods. Artistic creation appeared to reach its height in a quasi-somnambulist state of grace, an instinctive surrender to a *je ne sais quoi;* and meanwhile the critic strayed along those pedestrian paths which lead all around the arcanum but never into it.

Far from denying the reality of the conflict, I would doubt that it can be reduced to a simple disjunction. These age-old enmities between artist and critic, their historic quarrels and recriminations, are perhaps but an outward reflex of a perennial dialogue within the mind of the artist himself. For however much his creative impulse may resent the critical acumen by which it is tempered, this discipline is part of the artist's own craft, and indispensable to the exercise of his genius. In the end, we may well wonder whether these two irreconcilable foes—the artist creating *Where Angels Fear to Tread* and the critic anatomizing *Aspects of the Novel* —might not possibly be the same person.

Nor is it safe to infer, because the intellect assails the imagination, that a victory in this battle must entail a defeat. By innumerable variations of strategy, the creative and the critical moods of an artist may counteract or sustain or supersede one another, but we know also of those sublime instances in which they interpenetrate completely, as in the learned works of Raphael or Mozart, where grace and intelligence are one. Undeniably, there are cases where the two functions part; but here again, it is not a foregone conclusion that the artist who obliterates his intellectual awareness and surrenders to a kind of self-propelling instinct, achieves in that moment a higher demonstration of his powers. Leonardo's notebooks abound in drawings in which he allowed his hand to "doodle," performing motions over which his mind did not exercise a conscious control. There is general agreement that the figures produced in this instinctive manner are far inferior to those over which he watched with analytical care. And the same is true (to choose a radically different case) of Blake's hallucinations. The drawings he made directly from visions (we have no reason to doubt his own testimony) bear the marks of automatic transcripts; they look like tracings and are less expressive in outline than those which he perfected by conscious labor.

If then it is true, as these examples seem to suggest, that criticism can be a creative force in the very making of a work of art, it is not surprising to find that the finished work embodies a critical canon. This canon defines the aesthetic rules by which the particular work is to be judged, but in so doing, it implicitly reflects on the canons adopted by other artists. There is thus a persistent contention in progress, a "battle of the books," as Swift so happily put it, or in Hogarth's words a "battle of the pictures," a great *paragone* which in the field of music as well divides composers into camps and factions. While the polemical labeling of these camps may be a comparatively recent custom (so far as I know, it has been a fairly regular practice only for the last three hundred and fifty years), the cause for these divisions is far from frivolous. If the artist is an intelligent craftsman, he will want to explore the principles of his craft; and it is only natural that those "rules" and "devices," once the guarded treasure of cautious guilds, should be debated with dialectical zest by a liberally emancipated profession.

A work of art is thus loaded with critical matter, with technicalities to agitate the grammarians. And I hope I am not disrespectful in suggesting that every artist of stature harbors within himself not only a critic but one or two hidden grammarians as well. But when these come to the fore, the battle may deteriorate into an argument about syntax, a travesty of Balzac's "Comme un sentiment est logique!" The work of art then becomes a specimen that is prepared for inspection by the curious, and proves readily acceptable to professional botanists who divide the specimens into classes, arrange each class as a perfect series, and discover that each member of the series produces new members by a mysterious form of parthenogenesis.

But fortunately works of art are not made for artists alone, nor (which would be worse) for historians of art, but for a public on which they have an immediate, occasionally a profound, and at times a radically disturbing effect. They intrude into our so-called normal life, upset our standards, confuse our perspectives, arouse emotions we never knew, ignore sensibilities we have learned to cherish. In short, art is a vital form of interference, a "nuisance" which, if carried far enough, may extend even to the sacred regions generally entrusted to men of affairs and which are hence supposed to be well-secured against any inroads by the imagination. If I understood my assignment correctly, it is this mischievous nature of art, its role as a critical *enfant terrible*, which was primarily intended by the title of this paper. I shall attempt to do it justice, but I am afraid that this will lead me into offending some of the idols of the schools.

We have all been told by our aesthetic masters that the artist transfigures whatever he touches, that the all-too solid matter of this world melts away in the crucible of artistic creation. We have been promised, if only we submit to the conjuror's spell, that he will remove us from all terrestrial concerns and leave us transfixed in the contemplation of an ideal figment, which we can retain in its purity only so long as we allow it to subsist in perfect isolation. It is awkward to disturb such a happy dream; but idealism in matters of art has a family resemblance with its more common sister—it tells the truth, but only half of it. No one would wish to deny the strictly aesthetic qualities of a work of art, or to detract from its cathartic power. But while it is true that the artist transfigures our sensations, it is equally certain that they are also intensified by him. Consequently, the work of art has the power not merely to purge but also to incite emotions, to arouse a higher sense of awareness which may far outlast the artistic experience and become a force in shaping our conduct.

When Baudelaire wrote his prefaces to *Les Fleurs du Mal*, he protested in vain that this book was but an innocent exercise, designed to demonstrate how an exquisite artistry can transfigure an offensive theme. While he derided the vulgarity of those scribblers who make it a business "to mix up ink with virtue" ("à confondre l'encre avec la vertu"), his own desire to mix up ink with vice and infuse a poetic glory into evil, entailed commitments which he did not care to evade: "Le sujet fait pour l'artiste une partie du génie, et pour moi, barbare malgré tout, une partie du plaisir." The most sophisticated of poets, "barbare malgré tout," thus conceded his affinity to a savage. Like a primitive chieftain, he sensed that he could mold the conduct of a tribe by the sheer force of an incantation.

For the "critical nature of a work of art," this barbaric strain is of the utmost importance; for it invests the artist with a unique power to sting. There is no appeal against a verdict clad in a song. Hence the insouciant vitality of polemic art as illustrated, for instance, in Heine. In a political fantasy, which he called *Ein Wintermärchen,* he warned the king of Prussia that if he did not rescind his reactionary policies, he would write a poem in the manner of Dante's *Inferno,* where the king would find himself roasting in hell. And Heine took this occasion to inform the king that the hell of the poets is far more terrible than the fires prepared by theologians; for no god can redeem those who are incarcerated in Dante's awful tercets (*schreckliche Terzetten*).

Theologians, it is true, have made equally extravagant claims for their own doctrine of eternal damnation, but even the most orthodox would have to admit that there has been an occasional exception. The emperor Trajan, a pagan and hence unbaptized, was at first quite fittingly placed in hell; but when St. Gregory read of his singular merits, and realized that these could not save him from perpetual languishment, he was so moved by pity that he began to cry, and his tears served as a posthumous baptism, by which the emperor was cleansed and released. But even St. Gregory might find it difficult to rescue anyone from the *Inferno*. The perfect cadence of the poet's phrase, the precision and vigor of his image, impress themselves upon the memory of men, from which they cannot be dislodged. From great art there is no redemption.

If this is true, the poet's "singing flames" may prove a very perilous way of dispensing justice; for there is no certainty that his power of expression is always matched by his power of insight. Beauty is not always Truth; and when it becomes the vehicle of falsehood or error, it endows them with an attractiveness which the imagination of centuries may be unable to resist. To this day, for example, it is proper to think of Lucrezia Borgia as a kind of incestuous monster. Yet, as a matter of plain historical fact, Lucrezia Borgia was modest, well-behaved, and inclined to be humble rather than assertive. She was a faithful wife and an affectionate mother. As duchess of Ferrara, she was respected and beloved, and sufficiently versed in the art of government to serve as a competent regent in the absence of her husband. Altogether her conduct was so irreproachable that Ercole d'Este's rather critical ambassador could only report that she was somewhat colorless. How then did this fantastic legend originate? It was the invention of a poet—Sannazzaro. The Aragonese, engaged in a good political quarrel with the Borgias, were not satisfied with fighting them on the battlefield. They also enlisted in their service this most excellent of Italian versifiers, who wrote epigrams so vicious and at the same time so brilliant that even the skepticism of Guiccardini could not resist the poetic contagion. The infection spread as far as the nineteenth century, when Victor Hugo wrote a drama, Donizetti composed an opera, and Rossetti painted a picture of Lucrezia Borgia, all of them glorifying her legendary vices.

Against this conspiracy of the arts the truth proved powerless, even though temporal interests were no longer served by the fiction. The polemic point had completely vanished. Only the aesthetic image remained. In vain did a succession of meticulous scholars—Roscoe, Campori, Gregorovius—attempt to explode the fable. It was left for John Addington Symonds, the celebrated historian of the Italian Renaissance, to obscure their efforts by a dazzling somersault. Determined to show that he could fly like a poet along an elegant curve, and yet land on his feet like an historian, he placed the evidence squarely before the reader, explaining that "history has at last done justice to the memory of this woman"; but as he elaborated the theme, the poet got the better of him, and he concluded his account with the Pythian remark: "It is even probable that the darkest tales about her are true."

Les dieux eux-mêmes meurent,
Mais les vers souverains
Demeurent
Plus forts que les airains.

It might be argued that there is a simple remedy for these abuses. Why not plainly separate fiction from fact, and let each of them reign in its proper sphere? Let Victor Hugo declaim, and Donizetti sing, and Rossetti paint their figments. There can be no harm in their distortion of the truth, as long as we understand this to be *poetic license.* Meanwhile, truth can proceed on its sober path, unperturbed by the rage of poets.

The remedy sounds plausible enough in the abstract, but the pity is that it will not work. When imagination and understanding are applied to the same object (as they often happily are), they cannot fail to reflect on each other. Sannazarro's epigrams acquire a new facet of wit by our knowing that he was a liar, but the effect of Hugo's oratory is impaired if we begin to question his good sense. In other words, what we *know* about Lucrezia Borgia, has some influence on what we are willing to *believe* about her, and affects even our acceptance of *make-believe.* And conversely, the fancies with which artists have filled our minds cannot be banished by an act of will or safely quarantined when we begin to think in earnest. Nor is it desirable that it should be otherwise. The cure proposed, if it were effective, would produce a really fatal disease, a kind of schizophrenia, in which the intellect ignores what the imagination pictures, and the imagination disregards what the intellect knows; both functions helplessly coexisting in a distracted mind.

But even at its best, as a brief of freedom, an absolute grant of poetic license would fatally narrow the scope of art. It would reduce art to the level of an irrelevant pastime, a pleasant caprice unrelated to any basic impulse, suited perhaps for embellishing our leisure, but quickly forgotten when we settle down to serious business. The artist would be thus deprived of his greatest function, that of an explorer who can widen the understanding by probing into those darker respositories of experience which are not directly accessible to the intellect, and yet are indispensable to its working.

While the power of art to shape our judgment is quite unmistakable when the aim of the artist is avowedly polemic, we have seen that the polemic intent can vanish and the infectious process continue unimpaired. The image exerts by itself a kind of barbaric fascination. And the same applies, I believe, to the power of pure music, that is, to an art which no longer depends on either words or images to arouse our passions, but on sounds and rhythms alone. It might seem, indeed, that pure aesthetics would be safe in this particular field. But despite the detachment of sounds from things, the artist retains even here his peculiar capability to affect our understanding and mold our conduct. Let us suppose we had never heard Sarastro speak or sing, but knew Mozart's music only in its pure form, in chamber music or symphonies. Would it not be permissible to argue that the particular kind of sensibility and attention which is developed by listening to these works, has a natural affinity with the humane morality of Sarastro? Though not verbally equivalent to Sarastro's philosophy, the music of Mozart may perhaps be said to be favorable to a similar blending of rationality with compassion, and of relentless penetration with good humor and wit. And conversely: Do we require the verbal ejaculations of Tristan to sense that Wagner's music, by itself, has a raw potency of emotion which, if regularly inhaled, may prove singularly conducive to those pungently amorphous processes of thought which are characteristic of Wagner's heroes? The answer depends upon whether or not we admit that even in the evasive realm of musical expression there are certain limits of compatibility, so that a man who has trained himself thoroughly to feel like Tristan, may find it impossible to think like Sarastro, assuming that he concedes Sarastro to think at all.

And so we are back at the old battle of the Muses and the Sirens, and may have to decide which of the two parties we are to serve: the Muses who are so difficult to court, or the Sirens who make us so easily their prey. Certainly, to enter this battle is to become exposed to both; and possibly we must know the Siren before we can recognize the Muse. At least this seems to have been the opinion of Plato when he rebuked the Spartans for subjecting their youths to the hardships of pain, but not to the hazards of pleasure: "And those who drink from these two sources at the right time and in the right measure will be blessed . . . but those who do not, will be otherwise."

But what are the right time and the right measure? This is a question which, Plato insists, the artist should not be permitted to decide for himself; for if art were allowed to follow its own impulse, free from the restraints of a judicious control, it would produce bedevilment in us and around us, releasing the anarchic forces on which it plays. In Plato's view, the artist can transform us into whatever he pleases; and if given free scope, will use his power to the full. By the proper choice of modes in music, he will make us alternatively heroic and cowardly, harsh and pliant. By the use of suitable words, he will persuade us that bad things are good, and good things are bad, like the worst of all possible sophists. By inventing weird characters for a mime, he will make us relish them as dramatic parts, and induce us to adopt their objectionable manners until we are transformed by the playful force of imitation; for there is an insidious sorcery in so-called innocent games. In the words of James Harris, the Platonist: "What began in fiction, terminates in reality."

To modern ears, this indictment of the artist sounds a little frenzied in its fear. Having retained some of our Latin schooling and forgotten most of our Greek, we are always ready to acknowledge the *genius* in an artist without suspecting that this may be a *daemon*. Plato knew better. With Alcibiades among his elders, he saw witchcraft emanating from an artist turned statesman, and he witnessed the ensuing disaster. But the phenomenon is not purely Greek. Bolingbroke was English, yet he felt himself—possibly made himself—a reincarnation of Alcibiades. And is there anything extravagant in the suggestion that this plastic power, working a ruinous enchantment, is essentially that of the artist? Perhaps there is more truth than we care to admit in Plato's enigmatic warning: "When the modes of music change, the fundamental laws of the State always change with them." Obviously, an artist must be very great to produce such a profound effect; and this is precisely Plato's opinion. The greater the artist, the more he is to be feared. No witchcraft ever issued from a feeble imagination.

Modern legal opinion has not taken to Plato's conclusions. When a work of art is indicted in court for having a demoralizing effect, a not uncommon judicial procedure is to enquire whether it has any artistic merit; and if it can be established that it has, its innocence is regarded as proved. The practice is, of course, only to be applauded, for it tends to keep artists out of jail; but the reasoning is exceedingly faulty. It forgets that art intensifies what it transfigures, and that a great artist can do more harm than a little one. Plato was far more circumspect: "And if any such man will come to us to show us his art, we shall kneel down before him and worship him as a rare and holy and wonderful being;

but we shall not permit him to stay. And we shall anoint him with myrrh and set a garland of wool upon his head, and shall send him away to another city."

This is the most bewildering point about Plato's "fear." Animated by an unfailing sensibility to art and by an extreme estimation of its power, he is driven to conclusions which seem treacherously close to the reforms envisaged by Anti-Vice Crusaders whose fear is nourished by ignorance. It would be tempting to treat the two cases as one; for this would quickly rid us of the entire problem, and we could peacefully return to pure aesthetics. But there are some difficulties about throwing Plato into one category with Anthony Comstock; for Plato proposes reforms not exactly in keeping with the character of an abstemious moralist. While he aims at arousing in us a "divine fear" ($\theta\epsilon\hat{\iota}os$ $\phi\delta\beta os$) so that we may not be unduly swayed by a poetic incantation, he is scornful of what he calls a "limping virtue" ($\chi\omega\lambda\grave{\eta}$ $\dot{\alpha}\nu\delta\rho\iota\alpha$), a state of mind so hardened against the influence of art that it is no longer exposed to its dangers. He suspects that this failing creeps in with advancing age, when men have ceased to be carried away by their passions and begin to enjoy that righteous sense of security which is even blinder than passion itself. For this ailment Plato has a radical cure; he advises old men to get drunk, so that they may be newly exposed to the dangers they have forgotten, and rejoin the chorus of the young.

Plato's fear of art is thus counterbalanced by his abhorrence of the "limping virtue." To instill the fear without acquiring the limp, this appeared to Plato as such a difficult task, and so vitally important for the body politic, that he believed it would be necessary to invest the magistrate with the power to regulate, control, and censor. But this counsel of despair is so remarkably unpersuasive that one is inclined to suspect that it never quite persuaded Plato himself. He implicitly admits that the magistrate cannot be safely entrusted with this function unless he happens to be omniscient; and given this miracle in Plato's premise, our conclusion of course is a commonplace: As long as magistrates are not omniscient, we had better not entrust them with such powers.

But while we reject Plato's utopian remedy, I wonder whether we can afford to disregard his diagnosis. We shall certainly not trust the infallibility of our magistrates. But should we risk the confusions of blind chance? And if not, to whom are we to assign the role for which Plato required an omniscient legislator?

This role, I think, should be assigned to that most fallible of men, the critic. It is he who, in pronouncing on a work of art, should instill into us a sacred fear or castigate our limping virtue. And if he errs, as he must, there are other critics to rise up against him, and there is the artist himself who can produce a new work to confound the critic and force him to recant. For we are in no need of a final verdict. A sense of awareness is what we require. But that sense of awareness will not develop if criticism is confined to the quality of artistic workmanship, and is not allowed to extend to those human commitments which the workmanship cannot fail to entail. According to the doctrine of the autonomy of art, there is only one question which a critic may legitimately discuss: Has the artist achieved the effect at which he aimed? But I would argue that he should also ask the forbidden question: Should this kind of effect be aimed at, and what should be its place in our experience?

The habitual evasion of these issues shows not only a want of spirit; it is also very imprudent, and has in fact led in the recent past to a number of curious inconveniences. A few years ago, the hallway of Rockefeller Center in New York was to be decorated with frescoes. Mexican frescoes were very much in fashion, and the commission was given to Rivera. Presumably, those responsible for this choice were not unaware that Rivera held opinions which, if acted upon, would slightly alter the function of Rockefeller Center. But as they were dealing with art, they were animated by superior sentiments and willing to accept a decorative edification regardless of its import. In other words, they placed their trust in a limping virtue. But when Rivera's frescoes were completed, they proved too embarrassing to be retained. Without wishing to seem facetious, I would suggest that in having these frescoes removed, the liberal-minded patrons paid the artist a greater tribute than by commissioning them. Somewhat belatedly they had begun to fear that his art might convey his convictions.

A precisely converse dilemma arose at Dartmouth College, where frescoes were ordered from Orozco. In this case, no fear of the artist's power prevailed, in spite of the relentless violence of his message and the ferocity of his designs. The frescoes decorate a room in the Baker Library, where students are expected to sit quietly and read, unperturbed (I presume) by the revolutionary phantoms attacking them from all sides. A more solid faith in the ineffectuality of art is difficult to imagine; and the result is that this room is pervaded by a glacial atmosphere which deprives it of any living function. Officially it is called a "reserved book room," but the students are permitted to remove books if they prefer to read them elsewhere, which they are sensibly inclined to do.

These two extremes—iconoclasm and dereliction—are likely to occur when the fear of art either awakens too late or has vanished altogether. In the interest of a living art, it is essential to retain a sense of the risks involved in artistic expression; and this is to recognize the human force behind the aesthetic disguise. It might be objected that an extension of art criticism beyond the accepted boundaries of art would be a threat to artistic freedom; for the artist would be held responsible for acts which are imaginative and therefore noncommittal. But the association of the imaginative with the noncommittal is a cardinal fallacy in aesthetics, and a cause of irrelevancies in art. The critic might help to cure these failings by attacking them at their source. Unquestionably, a debate about human commitments might prove more awkward, and possibly more violent, than one confined to pure sensibility; but as a disciple of Machiavelli put it: "Those who want God to reside in their house, must admit the devil into the ante-chamber."

THE PERFORMER AS CRITIC

Olga Samaroff

IT IS with considerable trepidation that I invite this distinguished company to descend from the intellectual heights upon which such brilliant discussions of the aesthetics of art and criticism have taken place to the level of practical day-by-day musical criticism in the daily press and its effect upon music and musicians. In proceeding thus from the general to the particular, I must ask the indulgence of my audience if a part of this paper is devoted to personal experiences which form the basis of my conclusions.

In the *Gesammelte Schriften*[1] of Franz Liszt, we find the following paragraph, which I quote in an English translation:

Criticism should become more and more an activity of productive artists. In regard to the objection that an artist could not esaily undertake a dual activity, we assert that the function of the critic would have great value for the artist because through the evaluation and comparison of the work of others, as well as the résumé of decisions concerning them, every artist would inevitably gain in the maturing of his reflections and the logic of his ideas.

[1] *Gesammelte Schriften* (1855), IV, 138.

These words greatly influenced my decision to become music critic of the New York *Evening Post* in December 1925.

It required courage for a musician with no journalistic experience to follow such writers as Ernest Newman and Henry T. Finck in the columns of an important New York paper. But for an accident to my left arm which had forced me to cancel all engagements as concert pianist during the second half of a busy season, I should have been unable to consider the offer of the New York *Evening Post*. When Franz Liszt expressed confidence in the ability of a "productive artist" to combine the duties of the musical profession with those of a music critic, he knew nothing of the nature of a twentieth-century transcontinental concert tour in the United States, nor of the strenuous activities of the music critic of a New York daily newspaper in 1925.

When I actually read an announcement dated December 26th, 1925, the headlines of which read as follows: "Samaroff joins staff of New York Post. Noted artist engaged as critic to make her debut January 1st," I realized that the nervousness I had experienced before my debut as a concert pianist seemed, in retrospect, but a negligible sample of my capacity in the direction of panic. A subtitle in the headlines read: "Is adapted for work." This brought to my agitated mind the query, "Am I?"

The first paragraph in the body of the article constituted a still more formidable challenge: "It is·the first time in the history of musical criticism in the United States that a concert artist of Mme. Samaroff's rank and distinction has undertaken such work." I quote these lines in defiance of a very real modesty which would prompt me to refrain from doing so because the announcement of the New York *Evening Post* defined the professional circumstances which, I believe, explain the honor of the invitation I received to contribute a paper to this important Symposium under the title "The Performer as Critic." The word "professional" might profitably be added. I also assume that in view of my experience on both sides of the footlights, as it were, it is fitting for me to dwell somewhat upon the relation of criticism to musical performance.

If the works of the composer are to mean more to humanity than symbols on paper their adequate and continued performance is indispensable. The executant brings music to life. The fact that this element of performance is so important has brought into being a huge industry, and a relatively new one. The institution of public concerts only began to take shape during the eighteenth century. Opera has a longer history, but until the nineteenth century the art of criticism was primarily devoted to the composer of music. Today it is largely devoted to the performer, and while the great composer has survived a well-nigh continuous comedy of errors in the matter of evaluation of his works by fellow musicians, as well as professional critics throughout the known history of the art, the performer to whom critical appraisal means artistic life or death, as well as bread and butter, finds himself rather in the position of a prisoner at the bar every time he appears in public.

The first thing I did as music critic of the New York *Evening Post* was to publish a credo. Among the tenets it contained are two that furnish a point of departure for this discussion. They not only express my convictions of twenty years ago, but still hold today. I believe they are shared by most professional musicians engaged in the public performance of music. I wrote: "I confess that I possess no belief in musical criticism as a tribunal before which musicians are tried." The other tenet to which I allude was the belief that musical criticism should be regarded by all concerned—critic, artist, and public—as what it really is, "The impressions and opinions of an individual." Were it not for my knowledge of the mental attitude of the average reader of musical criticism, this truism would never have found its way into print in my credo. I had, however, learned enough of the practical results of music criticism during my career as a concert pianist to be aware of the general attitude of the public and the managers toward the pronouncements of music critics. A certain degree of infallibility always has been and still is attached to praise or blame dispensed by music critics in the daily press. The professional performer advertises the praise and resents the blame. The concertgoer usually buys tickets because of critical praise. As a rule, he is not inclined to spend his money on the concerts of performers who have been pronounced inferior by the critics of leading daily papers.

Orchestra conductors holding important positions have been made and unmade by critics—particularly in New York. Careers for hitherto unknown artists have blossomed overnight because of one strong paragraph so categorically worded as to leave no doubt in the minds of otherwise uninformed readers (as well as those of sellers and buyers of artists), that the individual performer in question possessed superlative merit. It is this *immediate* and *practical* result of newspaper criticism that creates such a terrific responsibility for the musical journalist.

When Maxwell Anderson recently brought up the same question in the field of the drama, Brooks Atkinson tried to disprove the crucial effect of criticism upon the fate of a play. He advanced some plausible arguments and impressive statistics. Nevertheless, Ward Morehouse, in the New York *Sun* of April 19, 1947, had this to say of the failure of *Message for Margaret* on Broadway: "There was only one Broadway opening this week—'Message for Margaret' . . . Well, it didn't do. Another instance of *a London success* running into trouble in New York . . . Stanley Gilkey co-producer of 'Margaret' accepts the defeat with good grace. He read the notices of a unanimously dissenting press and told his stars, Mady Christians and Miriam Hopkins, that class will be dismissed as of this evening." Ward

Morehouse performed a real service in providing an unequivocal documentary proof of the power of the press in relation to theatrical performance. It is true that some plays survive critical disapproval, as claimed by Brooks Atkinson. But that only occurs when producers refuse to accept defeat and hold on long enough for the public to make up its own mind.

It is very difficult for the individual professional performer of music to hold out. The indispensable general manager who sells artists to local managers throughout the country is inclined to accept defeat as Mr. Gilkey did when reviews are bad, just as he invariably recognizes the sales-value of good ones. The obvious reasons for this are purely practical. Nobody pays any attention to the general manager's evaluation of his own artists. His business interests would naturally incline him to pronounce them all geniuses of the highest order. He needs the expressed opinion of a recognized authority, and the only recognized authority whose evaluation can be used in such a way is the music critic of the daily press.

I learned this truth early in my own career as a concert pianist. Charles A. Ellis, then the most powerful manager in the concert field, told me that Philip Hale's evaluation of my piano playing had enabled him to offer me a contract. "Without something like that," said Ellis, "I could not sell a young and unknown artist like yourself." If a Charles A. Ellis could not sell an artist without a journalistic accolade, nobody could. As an educator of young pianists, I have learned that conditions have not changed in this respect except in a geographical sense. In my youth, the *European* accolade reinforced by critics of high standing in the larger American cities was required by the buyers of artists in the United States. Today the New York accolade has taken the place of the European—discontinued as the latter was during two world wars and at present, if only temporarily, still lost sight of.

The responsibility of New York critics weighed heavily upon me when I took up my duties as critic of the New York *Evening Post*. It caused me to examine and frankly to discuss the way in which this indisputable power of the press was being used. Whether or not I was the first "Performer as Critic" in the history of music criticism in the United States, I was—so far as I know—the first music critic who openly criticized criticism in the columns of a daily newspaper.

This, of course, was done in defiance of journalistic habits and customs. My stand was that if I undertook to criticize my musical colleagues there was no reason why I should refrain from criticizing my journalistic colleagues. To me a poor piece of criticism is on a par with a poor musical performance. The poor musical performance can temporarily damage the musical values of a composition, but the poor criticism can be lastingly destructive. By poor criticism I do not refer to literary quality. I mean something that is *factually incorrect*, or *factually unjust*. In a long study of music criticism the things I have learned to consider most detrimental to the prestige of the institution are:

1. A pretense of knowledge the writer does not possess.
2. The prejudice or cynical carelessness that lies at the root of most factual injustice. Examples of factual injustice which actually occurred during my tenure of office as critic were such things as the unfavorable review of a tenor at the opera, who because of illness had been replaced by another singer; a spuriously authoritative comment upon a performance or part of a performance by a critic who had not been present; and an adverse review of an entire concert which never took place.

These were some of the things I unhesitatingly criticized in my *Evening Post* column.

Naturally, this unconventional proceeding brought down wrath upon my head. The most serious manifestation of antagonism grew up within my own paper. Because of my journalistic inexperience an assistant had been assigned to write my headlines and help me edit the weekly music page. He happened to be a dyed-in-the-wool reactionary journalist who bitterly resented me and my unconventional attitude. My copy, which was trustingly sent in longhand to the *Post* every morning by messenger, went through his hands. He tampered with my script, wrote incredibly incorrect headlines, and caused me endless worry because of such errors in printing as the substitution throughout an entire article of the title of a composition which had *not* been performed for the one on the program. This, of course, was done to create the impression that I had not been present at the concert. It was at this point that I realized I had an implacable enemy rather than an ignorant assistant at work. This incident is worth mentioning only because it afforded startling proof of a journalistic psychology that provides sanctuary for the music critic. Nothing that appears in the columns of a newspaper should be questioned according to such a code. I am forced to assume that this psychology was the cause of my assistant's attitude and actions. I hasten to add my conviction that there are not many journalists who would have resorted to such unethical methods of expressing resentment. This experience was probably an isolated case.

Mr. Samuel Chotzinoff was then music critic of the New York *World,* and like myself a newcomer in the field. He had approached his task with maximum severity, while I followed a psychology born of my experience as a performer. My critical attitude might be likened to that of a lover of nature who can find beauty in a wild flower without any question of a comparison between its humble loveliness and such majestic natural phenomena as mountains or the sea. My tendency was to seek for the best in a sincere effort, and recognize whatever degree of merit it possessed. When I found some-

thing utterly unworthy I seldom wrote about it. Some-
how I could not feel that my readers would be particularly interested to learn that Miss Susie Simpkins
sang off-pitch and had not scaled the heights or plumbed
the depths of masterpieces she had attempted to interpret. Nor did I conceive it to be my duty to educate
the Susie Simpkinses. I went as often as possible to the
concerts of young or unknown musicians but if the performance was thoroughly bad, lacking even a modest
degree of merit, I simply did not write about it. My
strong desire and constant objective was to interest my
readers in music and to make my columns as informative
as possible. Everything that I wrote was based upon a
certain respect for artistic achievement even in a modest
degree.

My failure to write about bad performance was one
of the things that caused the impression of a preponder-
ance of favorable reviews in my columns. Incidentally,
it aroused just as much resentment in the neglected
musician as an adverse criticism. Even the advertising
manager of the *Post* rebuked me for it. But I stoutly
refused to write about something simply because people
had paid for an advertisement in the paper. I maintained
that they had already received value for their money.
The paper owed them no more.

Mr. Chotzinoff followed a different line. His praise
was reserved for things above the timber line, and it was
thrown into effective relief by his well-nigh unremit-
ting condemnation of everything else. Shortcomings

(and who cannot find them, particularly in new works and young artists) afford such excellent subject matter for a balance of praise and blame.

Mr. Chotzinoff once devoted considerable space in an article to what he called my "indulgent attitude." Using Voltaire as an ally, he wrote, "It's a good attitude taking it all around and one of its chief characteristics is that optimism which made Pangloss declare in the face of the destruction of all he loved best that this is the best of all possible worlds."

I replied with some asperity in my column, after alluding to the severity with which Mr. Chotzinoff was then assailing most musical things within earshot:

"No wonder Mr. Chotzinoff writes as he does if—as is subtly suggested—he finds himself facing the destruction of all he loves best. If anyone has been dense enough to fail to find a great love of music in Mr. Chotzinoff's writings, this ought to set things straight. His article may even inspire in pessimistic bosoms the hope of the dawn of a better day when, with the present feverish activities of concert halls and that nefarious institution, the Metropolitan Opera Company, effectively silenced, the super-artists who have in some miraculous way been able to find complete favor with Mr. Chotzinoff will make super-music at long intervals on the lonely ruins of a once flourishing New York musical life."

Today Mr. Chotzinoff and I smile at our journalistic sparring. Our relation is most friendly. Twenty years ago our respective attitudes represented two schools of thought in our field.

During these and similar experiences I learned some curious facts. For instance, when the music critic whose writings are prevailing severe in the matter of censure bestows praise, his favorable review has a special value. It can make an artist. It can launch a composer. By the same token, if the critic who takes what Mr. Chotzinoff called "an indulgent attitude" writes an *unfavorable* review, the effect is devastating. I naturally found it necessary from time to time to turn thumbs down on something I considered bad but important enough to write about. In such cases—without any assumption of infallibility—I expressed my opinion unreservedly. One manager said to me, "When *you* write a bad review, it is a catastrophe." The more indulgent attitude, therefore, can still uphold high standards even though admitting the existence of modest degrees of merit.

The most interesting thing in connection with these two schools of thought in the field of music criticism is the reaction of the public. I have reason to believe it is the same today as it was twenty years ago. I first learned to know it by means of a forum I introduced after my contract with the New York *Evening Post* had been extended. On January 8, 1927, I announced a weekly Music Forum. I quote from the announcement:

"It is my conviction that the most valuable functions of a daily paper in connection with music are: 1) Information, 2) Stimulation, 3) Critical appraisal. Well-meant efforts to guide and purify public taste by incessant fault-finding have as a rule been accorded first place . . . This Forum will have departments devoted to the printing and discussion of contributions or questions sent in by musicians, the public, and music students. It will also contain a Review of Reviews."

Among the musicians who immediately responded with interesting contributions were Ossip Gabrilowitsch and Tullio Serafin, at that time conductor at the Metropolitan Opera. Incidentally, Gabrilowitsch devoted his article to the value of choral singing and gave high praise to the Harvard Glee Club and the leadership of Dr. Davison who had brought it to such a high point of excellence. Mr. Serafin eloquently urged opera in English.

Questions from students literally poured in. But the most enlightening letters came from laymen readers who often disagreed with me. From them I learned the melancholy fact that a great many people prefer and enjoy adverse criticism. In fact, to them the word criticism has just one meaning: censure. Such people seem imbued with the spirit that once crowded the arenas in which gladiatorial combats to the death took place. It is akin to the sadism which still attracts crowds to bullfights and cockfights. From time immemorial there have been human beings who enjoyed witnessing torture and death. Perhaps, in a milder form, the critical "roasting" of a musician satisfies this urge. The severe critic is therefore giving the public what most of it wants.

The fan letters I received as critic on the New York

Evening Post invariably arrived after I had written an *unfavorable* review. The most scathing *criticism* I ever received from a reader came from a man who complained that I had written favorable reviews for an entire week. "A good critic," he wrote, "is one who knows enough to find the shortcomings in music and musicians. Anybody can hear what is good." In addition to this brilliant piece of logic it was evident that the writer of the letter in question *expected* me to find some shortcomings by Wednesday or Thursday if I had bestowed praise upon musical performances on Monday and Tuesday.

It is a great mistake to assume that a music critic shows courage when he attacks the established composer, performer, or musical institution. Still less can he claim to be fearless when he assails the defenseless composer of a new work or a young and unknown executant. On the contrary, it requires courage to bestow recognition of merit whenever and wherever it seems to be due without carefully weighing the proportion of praise and blame necessary to the preservation of one's status as critic. The brilliantly censorious critic is the virtuoso of the profession, and no musical showman who yields to the temptation to play to the gallery can be more sure of applause than the music critic who can add wit to severity. This fact brings to mind one of the questions which I believe we are here assembled to answer according to the preliminary announcement of this Symposium which invites us to discuss ways and means to help "the new army of listeners by providing them with a greater number of competent guides and interpreters." Can musical criticism as practised today in daily newspapers add something significant to the dispensation of praise and blame which at present constitutes its major activity?

I should like to preface my own answer to this important question by a brief description of my final experience as a music critic. When Julian Mason, then editor of the New York *Evening Post* offered me a further three-year contract, I had arrived at certain conclusions which may be interesting in view of the purpose of this Symposium. I drew up a plan for the kind of department of musical criticism I wanted. It contained various features which seemed necessary to me. I list the most important:

1. I specified a continuance and extension of my Music Forum, including a Children's Corner especially devised for the stimulation of interest in the younger generation.
2. I asked for several assistants of high musical and cultural caliber to be chosen by me. They were necessary to the research work involved in conducting the expanding Forum. No one could do it singlehanded.
3. I asked for permission to invite leading personalities of the musical world to contribute articles replacing from time to time those I had previously

furnished on Saturday afternoon. This was designed to bring important musicians closer to readers of the paper.

The plan included other features too long to enumer-
ate here. Before submitting it to Julian Mason, I showed
it to Mary Louise Curtis Bok (now Mrs. Efrem Zim-
balist), whose father, Cyrus Curtis, then owned the
Evening Post. She at once perceived that it would involve a financial expenditure the *Post* would not easily
undertake. She liked the plan well enough, however, to
make the incredibly generous offer to place five thousand
dollars a year at my disposal for the duration of my contract, so that assistants, guest writers and research workers could be taken care of. For personal reasons, she
made the condition that I should not make this known
at that time. She advised me to tell Julian Mason that I
would furnish the entire department without any addition to the handsome salary I was receiving.

I did this, but unfortunately for the project, Mr.
Mason *did not like music.* He also did not like innovations. He objected to having so much importance attached to music, and he feared the effect of such a department as I had planned upon others. It might create
a dangerous precedent.

My plan was rejected and I refused to sign a three-
year contract under the old terms. I had already determined to devote my life to musical education and if I
could not accomplish something of that nature in the

columns of a newspaper, I decided to seek opportunity elsewhere.

Much as I have enjoyed the task of developing the talented young pianists who have been confided to my care, I could never have restricted my educational activities to piano teaching. My forum in the *Evening Post* had taught me how eagerly laymen were reaching out for musical knowledge. The field of listener education beckoned and I soon found myself in the midst of fascinating pedagogical problems. Laymen who knew absolutely nothing about music served as "guinea pigs" throughout five experimental years at the Juilliard School of Music. I learned much more from them than they learned from me. Finally I ventured forth with classes called Layman's Music Courses at the David Mannes School of Music and the Junior League in New York. When the project outgrew these facilities it was offered a home in the Town Hall. Under the new title "Listener's Music Courses" I shall begin my ninth consecutive season there next October. This type of listener education is not to be confused with so-called music appreciation of the kind that sedulously avoids technicalities and stresses association of ideas or stories about composers that anybody can pick off the nearest library shelf. Nobody can be taught to *appreciate* anything. Laymen *can* be taught to *hear* music with awareness. There is such a thing as a technique of musical recognition for the listener. To develop it is the most difficult kind of teaching I know anything about. It requires a new and special method of presentation. The needs of my *listener students* have taught me *that the radio and the phonograph have done for music what printing did for literature*. Music has become universally accessible. The discovery of printing, however, would have been of little avail without the spread of literacy. The musical equivalent of literacy is imperative today. The layman wants it. Everything that contributes to it is important.

In the past it was believed that no musical literacy was possible without some attempt at composition or performance. "Mere listening" was scorned. An army of what I sometimes call "mere performers," when arguing this point, constituted the major part of musical society. Millions of human beings who experienced no urge to play or sing have been hitherto considered hopelessly unmusical. As virtual outcasts because of musical illiteracy, they came no nearer to music than the dance hall and various utilitarian uses of musical sound.

It has always amazed me that many musicians, even though they may know the facts, seldom stop to think of the unique nature of our Western Art Music. They forget that none of the civilizations of antiquity produced equivalents of Bach and Beethoven. Today we can search in vain in China and India for a musical art treasure comparable to the one we possess. The enrichment of life through the experience of *hearing* our great music is something that cannot be overestimated, and it is undeniable that the twentieth century has brought this experience within reach of all who desire it. Here the music critic can best find his way to participate in building the future by knowing his readers as people.

It is through personal experience that I benefited so greatly by my brief excursion into journalism. I learned to respect the scope of knowledge required of a newspaper critic. I acquired firsthand knowledge of the difficult conditions under which he works. I learned to value more than ever before the musical scholars whose writings enabled me to broaden my own knowledge. Above all, I learned the importance of the spoken and written word to the layman listener. So many musicians belittle this. They assume that the emotional quality of music will reach any listener and that nothing else matters. Musicians who rely solely upon the emotional reaction of the listener forget that the sounds of music like the sounds of language have a meaning. To enable a listener to find that meaning makes our art music a thing of the spirit for those who hear it—not merely one of the senses.

Olin Downes rightly pointed out in his article on this Critics' Symposium, published in the *New York Times* on April 27th, 1947, that, "The greatest hope associated with the coming Symposium—at least in the mind of the writer—lies in the effect that the conclusions of these conferences may have on the minds of newspaper editors and the newspaper-reading public." Mr. Downes is right. One thing that is needed is more space for music. This remark is directed to the newspaper editors. Incidentally, in looking over my scrapbook before writing this paper, I was amazed at the amount of space given me in the *Evening Post*. I also blushed at the length of my articles. When I first began to write I was popularly supposed to have a ghost writer, but I am sure this erroneous supposition could not survive the number of words it took to say what I had to say. No self-respecting ghost writer would have betrayed the literary inexperience which obviously caused this particular feature of my work. But it was truly phenomenal that the *Evening Post* gave me such unlimited space. As current paper shortage disappears I hope our musical columns of the present day will have similar possibilities of expansion.

As for readers, I repeat, some way must be provided to find out what is in their minds in order to meet their needs. In my opinion there is no better way than a forum such as the one I suggested to the New York *Evening Post* twenty years ago. The idea that everything educational is rejected by the American public is gradually disappearing. Radio quizzes have become popular. No music critic could undertake a classroom type of listener education, but well-conducted forums in a newspaper, with questions from the public carefully selected for discussion on the basis of general interest, could be infinitely more informative than any radio quiz. Two years ago I had a twenty-six-week radio hour every Sunday over Station WQXR in New York. The series was entirely built around questions from the public. Finally, prizes were offered for the best questions and suggestions for musically informative radio broadcasts. I enlisted the aid of two judges to assist me in sorting out the entries and awarding the prizes. One of these was Virgil Thomson. I was tremendously impressed by the interest he showed, the time he gave, and the trouble he took. No less impressive was his discerning judgment in handling the questions. What a brilliant forum he could conduct if the audience participation of his readers gave him positive knowledge of what they wanted to know, and how much better he or anyone else would learn to know the minds of the people who most need guidance through such a procedure!

Many fine men and women of unimpeachable integrity, unquestionable sincerity, and outstanding ability are today distinguishing themselves in the field of music criticism. Perhaps my idea of having guest writers in my proposed music department of the New York *Evening Post* might be worked out in a different way today. Why not have an exchange of leading music critics between the important papers of various cities? The *decentralization of music*, in the United States is under way. There is just one thing that remains static, and that is a certain psychological and commercial attitude towards music criticism in New York. Managers claim they cannot sell artists without favorable *New York* reviews. Hence the multitudinous debuts in that over-populated city. The New York critics probably have no desire to carry the burden of such a responsibility; the important general managers do not belittle the value of reviews in the papers of other cities; but I repeat, the *buyers of artists* today demand the New York accolade, as they once required that of Europe. The only thing that could eradicate this meaningless conventional idea would be an exchange of critics, and by that I mean that while New York critics would function temporarily in other cities, critics from those other cities should at the same time function in New York. It would interest me enormously as a reader, for example, to have a critic like Mr. Frankenstein review the New York musical scene for a fortnight, while Mr. Downes or Mr. Thomson performed the same duties in San Francisco. True, the *New York Times* and *Tribune* are read throughout the United States, but, apart from some factual news items and occasional articles of a general nature, Mr. Downes and Mr. Thomson naturally write about what takes place in New York. Through such an exchange as the one I have proposed, the capable and gifted critic could stand on his own merits regardless of the power of a particular paper in a particular city.

Guest conducting is the best avenue for building a reputation in the orchestral field. The guest critic could enhance his reputation and at the same time broaden his potential service to music by taking up temporary duties in different communities. As an outsider he would be free of local feuds and factions. If he found fine musical institutions in any community, his recognition of their merits would greatly strengthen them. Above all, he might help to alter the unsatisfactory status of the *resident* performer in our country.

The United States abounds in musical talent. Educational facilities of a high order are at the disposal of students, but the most gifted of our young performers dread the fate of establishing themselves as resident musicians in communities outside of a few large cities. Most of them want to stay in New York. The glamour and financial rewards of successful careers on the concert stage or in the opera house naturally attract them, but they are quite aware of the fact that many are called and few are chosen. If they could hope to find a stable professional life without the stigma of a certain inferiority which now attaches itself to the local musician, no matter what his attainments may be, I believe they would willingly turn in a direction which at present is resorted to only if everything else fails.

One of the greatest problems for the music critic is the correct appraisal of the new in creative music and the unknown in the field of performance. I once had a debate with Deems Taylor on the subject of music criticism before the Fortnightly Club of New York. When the question was asked: "Should young performers be encouraged or discouraged by the critic?" Mr. Taylor replied: "There are too many musicians, just as there are too many cats. Some have to be done away with." My answer was, "There have been so many glaring mistakes made by music critics throughout the known history of music that one could scarcely deny the danger of drowning the wrong cat." Creative genius of the highest order has always been rare in every country; but we cannot forget that in a nation of over a hundred and forty million people, all possessing, racially, some heritage from the old world, the amount of musical talent in the field of performance is too great to be absorbed by the musical industry as it is now organized. A wider field *must* be established. We cannot afford to plough under our musical talent.

Given space and opportunity by the owners and editors of newspapers, music critics could assume a most effective leadership in bringing about new conditions and wider opportunity for the professional performer's service to music.

When Dr. Burney wanted to hear Karl Philipp Emanuel Bach play the clavicembalo, Dr. Burney traveled to Hamburg. Burney could hear the compositions of Karl Philipp Emanuel Bach in London, but Bach was also famous as a performer and Burney wanted to hear him play. The point is, that as the institution of public concerts was in its infancy in the eighteenth century, the virtuoso performer had not begun to wander over the face of the earth. *Karl Philipp Emanuel Bach was a resident musician.*

The Barnum and Bailey methods introduced in America by Mr. Barnum at the time Jenny Lind first visited the United States, still prevail to a certain extent. Perhaps personal appearances of very great artists will always be demanded, but I am convinced that a return to the pre-nineteenth century conditions under which the most distinguished musicians *found a rich and valued professional activity as resident musicians* is the chief hope of our growing army of talented young American performers. We already have "composers in residence." As Harriet Johnson, now music critic of the New York *Evening Post*, proved in her illuminating survey of the American musical scene in the 1945–46 *Billboard Music Year Book*, we have an impressive number of orchestras, music schools, operatic workshops, and choral societies functioning throughout the United States. It now remains to stimulate excellence of quality in these musical enterprises and to attach such importance to those communities that can legitimately claim rank as a music center, that no musician, young or old, will regard working there as *exile*. Recording, radio (and eventually television), will enlarge the scope of the resident musician's activities, once his potential importance is based upon actual achievement, regardless of where he performs music.

In my opinion it is impossible to overestimate the potential power of musical journalism rightly used, in bringing these things about. Creative genius is an act of God. The critic can recognize a Beethoven or a Michelangelo. He cannot do more. But the level and the scope of the general practice of the art of music can be enormously influenced and even molded by those who wield the power of the press. After all, the art of music is one of the greatest and most unique artistic achievements of Western civilization. To serve music as an interpreter in our Western type of civilization is the highest function of the executant. To serve the art of music with discerning judgment, imagination, resourcefulness in the matter of imparting information, and true leadership is the highest function of music criticism in the daily press. In considering listener education as a new field inviting leadership and offering ever-widening opportunity to the music critic, I am reminded of a passage in *Prometheus Bound*. Aeschylus, in describing human beings before they received the gift of the divine fire, gives us food for thought in the following lines:

Eyes they had but saw not,
Ears they had but heard not;
Age on age, like unsubstantial shapes in vision seen
They groped at random in the world of sense.

THE ART OF JUDGING MUSIC *

Virgil Thomson

THE LAYMAN is under no obligation to exercise judgment with regard to musical works, to describe to himself their characteristics or to estimate their value for history. He can take them to his heart or let them alone. He does not have to be just or fair or to reflect about them in any way. He can accept, reject, or tolerate, using only caprice as his guide. The professional has no such liberty. Neither has any musical patron or amateur who has chosen to follow in his role of music consumer the standards that govern the music producer.

These standards are not immutable, but they do exist. They exist because being a professional involves, by definition, the assumption of a responsible attitude both toward the material with which the profession deals and toward society in general, which the profession unquestionably serves. That service, indeed, is the price of any profession's toleration by society. And the acceptance of money for professional services rendered is the criterion by which professionalism is determined in our society. This transaction is no guarantee of quality delivered, but it *is* a symbol of responsibility accepted. And once that responsibility is accepted, the workman must be at least morally worthy of his hire, however limited his skill or mental powers may be.

Every musician, therefore, is a music critic. He is obliged to make musical judgments and to act upon them. This necessity obtains primarily, of course, with regard to the work of other musicians, living and dead, in so far as his work is at all a comment on theirs or an interpretation of it (which nine-tenths, at least, of anybody's musical work is). And so even the composer, no less than the scholar, the pedagogue, the executant, and the reviewer, is constantly under the necessity of making a fair estimate, and a decently responsible one, of other people's musical work.

The first stage of this operation does not involve fairness at all. It consists of listening to a piece, or of reading it, rather in the way that a cook tastes food. This act of cognition, this beginning of acquaintance, is probably a more powerful determinant in our final judgments, the ones on which we act, than the subsequent cerebrations by which we endeavor to correct them. And we cannot prepare for it by purifying the spirit. We do not need to, as a matter of fact, because curiosity is stronger than prejudice. Any musician faced with a new piece will listen. He may not listen long but he will submit himself to it, if only for a moment. He will listen, in fact, as long as he can, as long as it holds his attention.

The second stage of the first operation, after the initial tasting, is going on listening—the experience of having one's attention held. Not all pieces hold one's attention. One is sad when they don't, but one must never undervalue the fact of their doing or not doing so. Fatigue here is of no more importance than prejudice. In reasonable health, and awake, any musician will listen to music, to sound of any kind, rather than merely ruminate, just as a painter will observe or an athlete move around. That is why he is a musician to start with, because listening is his line of least resistance. When a musician can't keep his mind on a piece of music, that fact must be considered when he comes to formulating judgment.

The final stage of the first operation is the aftertaste, the image that the whole piece leaves in the mind for the first few moments after it ceases to be heard (I say *heard* because reading a piece is hearing it in the mind, in however attentuated a fashion). This is as significant a part of its gustation as the first taste of it and the following of it through. It is a recalling of the whole, while memory is fresh and before the operations of correction and reflection have been undertaken. Never must one forget, never does one forget hearing for the first time a work that has absorbed one from beginning to end and from which one returns to ordinary life, as it were, shaken or beatified, as from a trip to the moon or to the Grecian Isles.

All new music does not produce this effect. But the degree to which it does is as valuable a datum for judgment as any that can be found in subsequent analyses. A great deal of subsequent analysis, as a matter of fact, is a search for the reasons why the piece did or did not hold one's attention on first hearing. And the initial taste or distaste for its qualities will constantly return to plague one's researches or to illumine them, to discourage or to inspire one in the process of making fuller acquaintance.

Making fuller acquaintance is the second operation of judgment. It depends, of course, on the success of the first. If first acquaintance has proved agreeable or interesting, one undertakes the second. The undertaking is a result of first judgment, though not necessarily of reflection. The whole first operation, let me insist, is spontaneous; and so is the initiation of the second. At this point, however, spontaneity ceases to be the main highway to experience, or guide to knowledge. We must now amplify and correct our first impression. If the first impression was gained from auditory means, from hearing only, we must now see the score. If it was gained from a score, we must now hear it in execution. Many pieces look better than they sound; and even more of them sound better on first hearing than their design justifies, because sound is usually pleasant whether or not high intrinsic interest of an expressive or textural nature is present. In the case of executant musicians there is a constant shifting, during the study of a work, between score and execution, each stimulating and correcting the other till the artist's interpretation is fully formed as a concept and completely clothed in sound.

At this point there is material for a reflected judgment, and one formulates that judgment if there is a necessity for doing so. Otherwise one continues to study and to correct until interest flags. The third operation of judgment can be undertaken only after a period of rest, of vacation from the subject. One has to forget the study period and its results, one has to approach the work all over again from a distance. Here the acquisition of experience and those shifts in the center of emotional experience that come from growing older are capable of lighting up the work in a new way. Sometimes they make it appear nobler and more interesting; sometimes they show up shoddy material or poor workmanship; sometimes one can't see why one ever bothered with the piece at all. As in reading old love letters or reviving an old quarrel, one's former association is now an element to be dealt with. It involves one in loyalty or ruthlessness, in any case in lots of remembering. The music is no longer new and shining; nor has it been kept bright by continual use. It has acquired a patina that must be rubbed away before one can see the object as anything like its old self. Re-study and rehearing are necessary if a new judgment has to be made. And a new judgment does have to be made if one is going to use the work again for any purpose whatsoever.

No judgment, of course, is ever final or permanent. At any stage of musical acquaintance action may become necessary; one may have undertaken to perform the work or to explain it to students or describe it in public. For any of these purposes one must formulate some kind of judgment—if not about its value, at least about its nature. This formulation can take place at any point.

Reviewers describe new music from one hearing, as pedagogues criticize student compositions from one reading. In nine cases out of ten this is quite sufficient for the purpose, and no injustice is done. Works of standard repertory are more often described after both hearing and study, that is to say, after the second phase of acquaintance; such acquaintance being easily available nowadays to all, though the press is not invariably as well prepared in standard repertory by score study as it might be. Furthermore, many members of the teaching profession do not have as broad a repertory as might be desired for the answering of student questions and for exposing to the young all the kinds of music that there are. The press in general tends to express judgments of new works from hearing only, just as music historians, especially those dealing with remote periods, are obliged to describe from score a great deal of music that they have never heard at all.

In order to make a fair judgment from only the first stage of acquaintance, either from hearing or from reading, everybody is obliged to have recourse to the aid of clues and clinical signs. The clinical signs of quality are (1) a certain strangeness in the musical texture; (2) the ability of a work to hold one's attention; (3) one's ability to remember it vividly; (4) the presence of technical invention, such as novelty of rhythm, of contrapuntal, harmonic, melodic, or instrumental device. The pattern that a score makes on a page can be enticing, too, even before one starts to read it. In the matter of attention, it is not germane that one should be either delighted or annoyed. What counts is whether one is impelled to go on listening.

It is necessary to keep wary, too, and to examine one's mind for possible failure to make the cardinal distinctions. These are (1) design versus execution, or the piece itself as distinct from its presentation; (2) the expressive power of the work as distinguished from its formal musical interest; (3) a convincing emotional effect versus a meretricious one. One must ask oneself always, "Have I heard a pretty piece or just some pretty playing?" "Has an abstruse work been obscured by the more facile character of its neighbors on the program?" "Have I been listening to sentiment or brilliance, counterpoint or profundity?" "Have I been moved or merely impressed?"

Study will provide answers to all these questions; but when one has to act quickly, one must assume that one's first impression, so far as it goes, is a true view. And it is, in fact, as true a view as any, since most of what is revealed on further acquaintance is of a descriptive nature, a more detailed picture filling in outlines already sensed. This is not always so; but far more often than not it is. In the case of successive contradictory impressions, it is the first, I think, that tends to survive.

First one votes about a piece, spontaneously, sincerely, and more often than not, permanently. One adopts it or rejects it. Liking is not necessary for adoption, but one must be interested. In that case one can study the work further with profit. In the other case one forgets it. After study one can forget it too, but not completely. In this case one can revisit it after a time. But at any time when the formulation of a judgment or opinion is found to be desirable, that formulation must be based on a description of the work. The techniques of musical description are:

1. *Stylistic* identification, its period or school, as recognizable from internal evidence, from the technical procedures employed. These answer the question, "What is it like?"

2. *Expressive* identification, its depiction of the cadences of speech, of bodily movements or of feelings (that whole series of anxiety-and-relief patterns that constitutes emotional life). This decodifying is a more difficult operation but also a more important one, since one can, if necessary, neglect stylistic differences or even abstract them from the problem, whereas one cannot perform, communicate or in any other way *use* a piece of music until one has found an answer, correct or incorrect, to the question, "What is it about?"

3. The classical aids to memory. These are the known methods of melodic, harmonic, orchestral, and formal analysis. They are of little value without stylistic and expressive identification, but they help one to remember detail, provided one has first understood the whole. George Bernard Shaw showed the futility of formal analysis without reference to content in a paragraph of program notes such as might be written about the most

famous of the Hamlet soliloquies. He begins, "The theme is first stated in the infinitive mood, followed immediately by its inversion." Analysis is an indispensable procedure, but the analysis of a given piece is valueless to anyone who does not have some previous knowledge of the work. That is why one must first, in describing a work, answer the questions "What is it like?" and "What is it about?" before attempting to answer "How does it go?"

4. The fourth procedure of musical description is the verbal formulation of it. This is, of course, a literary rather than a musical problem; but no one escapes it, not the teachers, the conductors, or the string-quartet players any more than the historians or the journalists. In some of the musical branches it is easier than others. Vocalism is particularly hard to teach otherwise than by example, or to describe in any circumstance, because there is no standard vocabulary for the purpose. Instrumental terminology is richer, though most of this is borrowed from the language of painting. Composition is chiefly described in metaphor, though the stylistic and expressive identifications do have a scholastic terminology. That for styles follows the history of the visual arts except for the years between 1775, say, and 1810, where the visual artists discern a neoclassic period and the musicians a Classical one (with a capital "C"). The classification of subject matter as strophic, choric, or convulsive is elementary; but the latter division, which includes so much of our grander repertory, is incapable

of further precision other than that available through poetic allusion. The same is true of musical landscape painting. Here one must use similes, there is no other way.

You will note that I have said nothing about communicating one's passion about a work. I have not mentioned it because it presents no problem; it takes place automatically and inevitably. What is most interesting about any musical judgment is the description and analysis on which it is based, or, if you like (since the judgment is likely to precede the analysis), by which it is defended. This is revelatory and stimulating. The fact that one man likes or dislikes a given piece will influence nobody. The fact that he considers that piece to be, shall we say, more like a newspaper editorial about something than a direct transcript of personal sentiments is, however—right or wrong, convincing or foolish—worth following up, if only for refutation.

Nobody has to be right. Any opinion is legitimate to act on provided one accepts in advance the responsibilities of that action. Any opinion is legitimate to express that can be stated in clear language. And any opinion at all is legitimate to hold. As I said before, it is not the yes or no of a judgment that is valuable to other people; though one's original yes or no may have been the determinant of a whole lifetime's activity. What other people get profit from following is that activity itself. That is why, just as an emotional reaction is more significant for its force than for its direction, a musical judgment is of value to others less for the conclusions reached than for the methods by which these have been, not even arrived at, but elaborated, defended, and expressed. Here is the terrain where a man's professional qualifications show up. The instinct for judging music is universal; acting on musical judgments is a privilege of the profession. The art of formulating musical judgments is chiefly the art of describing music. At this exercise it is desirable to be skillful and, as often as possible, convincing. But it is the skill that counts, the skill or gift, if you will, of understanding and explaining— at least of explaining that such and such is, for the present, one's understanding of the matter.

The foregoing is, for the present, my understanding of the chief procedures involved in the formation of musical judgments. The *formulation* of these in clear language is another subject. That belongs to the English department. It cannot, however, be neglected with impunity by musicians, since poor verbal expression can become as expensive a habit as poor judgment. That is why, when young people ask one how to prepare themselves for musical criticism as a profession, the double reply is obligatory: "Study music and learn to write."

CONSEQUENCES OF THE RECORDED PERFORMANCE

Otto Kinkeldey

IT IS as a historian that I come before you, and my thoughts and words concerning this Symposium are more or less influenced by historical considerations. It is quite evident from the variety and the contents of the papers and addresses which have been thus far presented to this audience, as well as from the numerous attendance at these conferences, that the problem of criticism in music has aroused great and widespread interest.

It would surely be wise for us to see that our understanding of the term, criticism, is sufficiently broad and all-embracing. We must repudiate the definition of those who understand by criticism a merely censorious, captious fault-finding. No genuine critic approaches his task in this spirit. And the problem of criticism is not restricted to the professional writer of music criticisms. If we keep reminding ourselves that we can use the word criticism as a synonym for judgment, we shall be safer. It is the problem of musical judgment in its widest sense, its exercise and its significance, not only for the professional critic but for the composer, the performer, and the hearer, that should be the basis for all discussions of music criticism. The excellence or the inadequacy of our composite musical, critical judgment determines the higher or lower level of our musical culture.

The place of the recorded performance in the formation of this critical judgment may be viewed from various angles. I shall venture to transgress, to a certain extent, the narrower limits of my specific assignment in this Symposium in order to bring a historical light to bear upon the subject. The historical approach would begin with an inquiry into the nature of critical musical judgment as it was, as it is, and as it may be in the future. An adequate treatment would go far beyond the purpose of this present address. But a few side lights will surely be of interest to all who think seriously about our problem.

There is first the realization that the idea of judgment in music has had a decided mythopoetic value. You are probably all familiar with the tale of the musical contest between the divine Apollo with his lyre and the flute-playing Marsyas. Midas, King of Phrygia, who had been appointed to judge the contest, awarded the victory to Marsyas. And here we have the first instance in history of the music critic criticized—and even punished. For Apollo and the Muses were not satisfied with the judgment of Midas and reversed it. The unsatisfactory critic was punished by being fitted out with a pair of asses' ears. Midas resorted to wearing a concealing cap; but he could not hide his shame from his barber. The barber, disquieted by his dangerous knowledge, sought to relieve himself by digging a hole in the ground, whis-

pering into it: "Midas has asses' ears," and then filling
the hole with earth. It was of no avail. The reeds that
sprang up on the spot proclaimed the secret to the whole
world. The role of the music critic in those days was
not without its dangers. In addition, the unfortunate
performer, Marsyas, was flayed, and thus paid for his
rashness in daring to compete with the great Apollo.

We have, as yet, no continued story of musical judgment or musical criticism in the Middle Ages or in the
Renaissance. What we need is a historical investigation
which will parallel the profound studies made in the
field of literary criticism. Literary scholars have been
keenly interested in the question of criticism, and great
men of letters have taken a hand in the discussion of
the problem. For the early centuries of the Christian era
the well-known treatise, *On the Sublime*, by Longinus
starts the line of a long series of critical works. In the
thirteenth century we find that the immortal Dante did
not scorn to turn his mind to the discussion of critical
problems. In more recent times we have, in English
literature, great critical writers in Samuel Johnson and
in Matthew Arnold. And for a careful and in itself
critical survey of the whole story we have the monu-
mental three-volume work of George Saintsbury, *A
History of Criticism and Literary Taste in Europe*
(1900–1904). A musical Saintsbury has not yet appeared. But we do have a recent work by Dr. Max Graf,
a Vienna music critic, entitled *Composer and Critic*
(1946), in which the music criticism of the last two

hundred years is discussed in some detail. Whether the book is itself susceptible of favorable or unfavorable criticism need not concern us here. It is at least an attempt to open up the history of the subject; but it can in no wise be compared to the profound and all-embracing work of Saintsbury.

That, because of the very nature of musical art and of musical production, the problem is much more difficult for music than for literature has been pointed out often enough, yet I do not hesitate to repeat the statement here, for it has a direct bearing upon the question of recorded performance. In fact, the historian of musical criticism will have to repeat a great many well-known facts. To shrink from the repetition would be to yield to that "horror of the obvious" which, as Saintsbury says, "bad taste at all times has taken for a virtue." The musical difficulty was recognized as early as the Renaissance. Leonardo da Vinci was no mean critic of art. In the *Treatise on Painting* ascribed to the great master we have an attempt to set up a ranking order of the various arts. Here painting comes first. Music is lower, chiefly because of its impermanence. "It dies as soon as it is born."

This is not true of music criticism as such. Critical opinions can be written down and thus share in the permanence of literary criticism. Still we have no great body of aesthetic and critical writing for music in the Middle Ages or in the Renaissance comparable with the music criticism of our own times or with the literary criticism of the Middle Ages and the Renaissance.

It is a fact not generally known that the music historian, Charles Burney, regarded the problem of music criticism as worthy of specific attention. Burney was a sharp critic of the music of his own time, not always just toward the musicians of his native land. But his theoretical principles were, on the whole, sound and practical. You will find them in his "Essay on Musical Criticism," packed away as the Introduction to the third volume of his *General History of Music* (1789). Since the essay is little known and should be of interest to such an audience as this, I feel justified in quoting several passages.

As music may be defined the art of pleasing by the succession and combination of agreeable sounds, every hearer has a right to give way to his feelings, and be pleased or dissatisfied without knowledge, experience, or the fiat of critics; but then he has certainly no right to insist on others being pleased or dissatisfied in the same degree. I can very readily forgive the man who admits a different Music from that which pleases me, provided he does not extend his hatred or contempt of my favorite Music to myself, and imagine that on the exclusive admiration of any one style of music, and a close adherence to it, all wisdom, taste and virtue depend . . .

There have been many treatises published on the art of musical composition and performance, but none to instruct lovers of Music how to listen, or to judge for themselves. So various are musical styles, that it requires not only extensive knowledge, and long experience, but a liberal, enlarged and candid mind, to discriminate and allow each its due praise. Nullius addictus jurare in verba magistri . . .

A critic should have none of the contractions and narrow partialities of such as can see but a small angle of the art; of whom there are some so bewildered in fugues and complicated contrivances that they can conceive pleasure from nothing but canonical answers, imitations, inversions, and counter-subjects; while others are equally partial to light, simple, frivolous melody, regarding every species of artificial composition as mere pedantry and jargon. A chorus of Handel and a graceful opera song should not preclude each other: each has its own peculiar merit; and no one musical production can comprise the beauties of every species of composition. It is not unusual for disputants, in all the arts, to reason without principles; but this, I believe, happens more frequently in musical debates than any other.

The question: "Sonate, que veux tu?" which Burney ascribes to Fontenelle, would never have been asked by a real lover or judge of music.

To a real lover and judge the Sonata should answer: "I would have you listen with attention and delight to the ingenuity of the composition, the neatness of the execution, the sweetness of the melody, and the richness of the harmony, as well as to the charms of refined tones, lengthened and polished into passion.

Here is Burney's reaction to some of the music of his own day:

The extraneous and seemingly forced and affected modulation of the German composers of the present age, is only too much for us, because we have heard too little. Novelty has been acquired, and attention excited, more by learned modulation in Germany, than by new and difficult melody in Italy. We dislike both, perhaps, only because we are not gradually arrived at them; and difficult and easy, new and old, depend on the reading, hearing and knowledge of the critic.

We must admit that Burney's theory of criticism, as far as it went, was sound. It is as valid today as it was a century and a half ago.

But let us bring our discussion a little nearer home and come closer to the narrower subject of our title. How does the modern invention of recorded music affect not only the critic but the composer, the performer, and the hearer? What are the historical implications of this new invention and how will it affect the future development of the art? Edison's first tin-foil phonograph was patented in 1877. We have had over half a century of real experience with recorded sounds, and we should be able to make deductions and draw conclusions from this experience.

Back of all thinking and discussion of the consequences of recording lies the basic problem of the relation of the artist to his public. How is any utterance in any art communicated by the creator to the recipient? The arts differ greatly among each other in this respect. I venture to recall to your minds the distinction often made between the so-called space arts and the time arts. The arts which exist in space, like painting and sculpture, work in mediums which give us a more or less permanent art product, the painting or the statue. The time arts are those which, as Leonardo said, die as soon as they are born. Music and the dance are such arts.

For music particularly, the immaterial existence, the evanescence, is a serious drawback. For each successive communication of the creator's message there must be a new re-creation; and the re-creation is in most cases the work of another artist than the original creator. The musical composer is almost always at the mercy of his intermediary, the performing artist. It is true we have had great composers who were their own interpreters. Bach, Mozart, and Beethoven often performed their own compositions in public. In more recent times we have composer-pianists like Liszt or Rachmaninoff. Violinists of this caliber are not as numerous. Great as was the impression which Paganini made upon his audiences, we would hardly call him a great composer. Great composers of vocal music who could interpret their own works are few and far between.

How vastly different is the relation of the composer to his public from the relation of a Greek sculptor, of a Giotto, a Michelangelo, a Watteau, or an Epstein to those who behold their works! The rise of a new science, or a new art, if you choose to call it so, of recording music bids fair to make a great change in this respect.

I have often indulged in a fantastic speculation as to what would happen if the composer of music were to be placed in the position of the painter or sculptor, if, in some way, he should be enabled to create his own musical work in a permanent form, which would require no reinterpretation, but which could be reproduced at will in exactly the form given to it by its creator. Although I have discoursed on this topic in the past to a Harvard audience and in other circles, I ask your indulgence if I repeat briefly some of the salient features of this flight of imagination.

The steady development of recording methods, not only on plastic discs but on the sound track of a moving picture film, and the new forms of sound producing and sound controlling electric instruments, should suggest that science might ultimately produce an instrument— a composing machine I should like to call it—which would place the whole realm of sound production directly and immediately into the hands of the composer. It would not require long years of technical practice such as are necessary to acquire the muscular coördination and facility that now go to the making of a virtuoso performer. Like the painter in his studio, the composer could work in peace and quiet at his own pace, making the desired combinations of tempo variation, of dynamic differentiation, far more subtle than those now possible to players of instruments, using tone colors in infinitely greater variety than is possible with the orchestra instruments of the present day. Even the human voice need not be left out of the picture; for we have already constructed machines which produce mechanical, synthetic sounds that can be interpreted as resembling human speech. Like the painter, the composer could make repeated trials and experiments until he was satisfied with the result. The final function of the composing machine would be to deliver a complex wave form like that which is now cut into a gramophone disc or photographed on a sound track. The line thus delivered could be recorded as at present or by some even more exact and adequate method, and the recording would stand for all time as the final utterance of the individual composer, to be reproduced at will wherever and whenever it was desired.

If the last stage of refinement and mechanical perfection for this ideal situation should ever be reached, the virtuoso orchestra conductor of today would probably disappear. The virtuoso performer as we know him would sink to the place occupied by the copyist in the arts of painting and sculpture, except when he was performing his own creations.

But the beginning has been made. We have taken the first step on this road. The science of recording has progressed so far as to make the performing artist wholly independent of the time element or the impermanence of earlier music production. The performer of today is often a creative (that is to say, re-creative) artist of the highest type. And this quality of his performance can now, within limits, be permanently preserved. Our reproductions are not perfect. Some sound effects are still beyond the power of the modern reproducing instrument. It cannot yet cope with the peculiar energy of a resounding thwack upon the bass drum nor of a pistol shot. There are still many in this audience who will remember the woeful sounds that came from the early wax cylinder recordings. It is not so many years since we recognized the percussive sounds of the piano only by their likeness to beating upon tin pans. But the sneers which met the earlier specimens of "canned music" have disappeared entirely. The recording laboratories are engaged in a ceaseless labor of improvement. The sound engineers of the film track still resort to the most ludicrous if interesting makeshifts for some of their sound effects. But with increasing perfection the soundtrack may ultimately replace the disc recording for musical purposes.

The other arts have not been slower than music to develop adequate means of reproduction. Think of the fascinating results of modern color process printing or of the color collotype. They cannot replace an original painting, but they offer a surrogate which for certain purposes is quite adequate. The study and the teaching of the history of art as we know them today would be utterly impossible without these reproductions. Musical recordings serve the same purpose in their field. Even if they had no other use than this, we should welcome the recording as an invaluable contribution to civilization and culture.

I shall recur to the historical aspect presently; but the question has much broader implications to which I should like to direct your attention. What is, or what is likely to be, the effect of the recording upon the broad faculty of musical judgment in the human race? Will our critical faculty be improved by the use of the new procedure? I think the answer must be decidedly affirmative. So far as judgment is the result of careful study and continued thought, with repeated observation, so far as a mental activity like the critical faculty can be developed, improved, and sharpened by practice and repetition, so far will the advent of the recording pave the way for the elevation of musical taste. Under the old dispensation the judge or critic was hampered by the difficulty of repeated hearing, except insofar as he was himself a performer. Freely repeated performance was somewhat difficult in the case of chamber music, and well-nigh impossible for orchestra music. We met the same obstacle when we attempted to judge the merits of a virtuoso performance as such. The art critic had no such difficulty. The dramatic critic could, in some cases at any rate, have recourse to the book of the play. For poetry, so far as it was meant to be heard, we could be our own performers.

The repetition difficulty in music bears most heavily upon the professional music critics of our daily papers. As Dr. Davison pointed out in the opening address of this Symposium, our newspaper critics are, or should be, the most important formers of musical taste in our modern musical life. But the exigencies of our daily press service require these most influential judges to be ready, after one hearing, with a considered judgment not only of a performer's merit or demerit, but of a composer's success or failure. There is not much time for deliberation or study. It is true, a newspaper critic often studies a score before hearing the work or the performance which he is to judge. This is not always possible with new works. Will the critic ever be able to study a recording of a new work before he hears it in the concert hall? Under present conditions this is not very likely. Commercial recordings are generally made only after a work has been fairly launched.

The newspaper critic of the present day must be a man of prompt judgment. He must, in a certain sense, be a lightning sketch artist. Among the brethren of the guild there are some who are undoubted virtuosos in this art, and one can easily imagine that they find a decided exhilaration in the exercise of this faculty. Mr. Virgil Thomson has expressed the opinion that, once we admit the need for a quick judgment for speedy publication on the part of the newspaper critic, there was little likelihood of a difference between the criticism written in two hours and a criticism written in two days. All this is based upon a system which counts upon one hearing only. But suppose that by some improved, relatively simple yet reasonably adequate recording device, like

the steel-wire method, it were possible to make a recording of an important new composition at the final rehearsal, would serious critics take advantage of the
possibility of repeated hearing and study of the work
before its official first public performance? Surely this
would afford them an opportunity to familiarize themselves with the actual sound of the work even better
than a score, and their ears and their minds would be
set for a more careful and considered hearing and judgment when the work was presented to the public.

Aside from this actual condition of present-day journalism, I believe that there are few critics who would
not take advantage, wherever it might be possible, of
recordings to familiarize themselves with newer works
for all except the "first performance." And surely, for
the critic and the music-lover alike, the recording affords
a means of arriving at a comparative judgment of the
renditions of the same composition by various performers, or of the varying interpretations of an orchestral work by different conductors.

Let me return briefly to the historic significance of the
recording practice. I run no risk of serious contradiction if I suggest that a sound musical judgment, liberal,
broad-minded and far-sighted, should rest upon a feeling
of historical continuity with the past development of
the art. I do not believe that there are many who would
insist on throwing the past overboard entirely, of obliter-
ating it forever. But it is not easy to know the musical
past, and it is still more difficult to restore it to life. Be-

fore the era of recorded music the only aids to continuity were tradition and written symbols on paper. Tradition in music is a very weak link—witness the difficulty of plainsong restoration. The written symbols are helpful only so far as we feel that we still have a traditional connection with the art expressed in those symbols, with its idioms of speech and expression, with the conventions and manner of performance, and even with the manner and conventions of hearing and apperception.

I imagine that most of us feel that the language and the expression of Johann Sebastian Bach are still within our comprehension. The idiom of Haydn and of Mozart is as easily intelligible to us as the language, let us say, of John Milton or Alexander Pope. But as for Palestrina we are not at all certain about the conventional sound of his music in his own day. And alas! for the epochs before Palestrina even the most learned musical scholar must confess that he can by no means be sure of how we should reproduce the works for which the written symbols have come down to us.

How different would be our position if the phonograph had been invented in the Middle Ages. What would we not give for a recording of a piece of plainsong sung in the time of Gregory the Great, or for a polyphonic piece by Perotin, a Mass by Machault or a Chanson by Dufay. As a matter of fact we never hear a Bach cantata, a Mozart or even a Beethoven symphony exactly as their composers heard them. Records, made in the times of these composers, would probably give us much to think about, if we compared them with the sound of their compositions as played today.

This applies to the quality of the performer's re-creation as well as to the intention of the composer, so far as the latter was able to control or to influence the performance of his work by another. From one point of view it is one of the less admirable features of the present attitude toward recorded music that for a very large portion of the record-buying public the name of the performer as given on the disc or in the catalogue looms larger than the name of the composer-creator. There has been, however, a notable improvement in this respect in recent years. But be that as it may, the historical significance of recordings for the preservation of virtuoso performances cannot be denied.

The younger members of the present generation who never heard Caruso sing can still gain an impression of his wonderful voice from existing records. No one now alive can tell us or show us what it was that overwhelmed the fanatical worshippers of the greatest of Caruso's near predecessors. The illustrious tenor, Mario, faded into the background in the 1860's. His voice is merely a myth to us. To practically all of us Mario is merely a name in a book.

Without recordings our modern music and the actual life given to it by the style of performance would be doomed to the same fate. Can you imagine what would happen in the absence of recordings if, three-hundred years hence, some one should dig out of a music library the printed, published, or the manuscript parts of some of the most popular jazz compositions of our day? I mean the real, hot jazz, which carries its votaries into the seventh heaven of ecstasy. If there were no recordings to perpetuate the actual sound and furnish a model for the performers of the future, I am sure that a modern jazz fanatic, revisiting the earth centuries hence, would stand aghast at the sounds produced by the players of that future age as they attempted to reproduce the music "from notes." No indeed! the advent of the recording will have a most profound effect, not only upon the development and the continuity of musical art alone, but of all those manifestations of the human spirit which depend upon sound as their medium of communication. The future will never know how an oration by Demosthenes or by Cicero sounded, but it may make itself quite familiar, if it chooses, with the oratory of Adolf Hitler.

Even in our own day we are beginning to realize the real meaning of this new form of artistic being. The commercial producers of recordings are beginning to take their business much more seriously from the point of view of musical art. The increasing numbers of re-productions of large, important works in the form of albums are finding a correspondingly increasing number of willing music-lovers who will buy the larger works. The importance of the recording development is being recognized. We have special journals devoted to the discussion of recorded music. A special group of critics of recordings has come into being. Bibliographical reports of new publications, special columns of record reviews and criticisms in some of the newspapers, all help to stimulate interest and to improve the taste of those who hear music in this form.

The question is often asked as to whether this progress in recording music does not have a marked general effect in raising the level of musical taste and culture for all men. On this point I fear that my own reaction would not be entirely pleasing to the ardent record enthusiast. It is happily true that the number of those who can now hear music is vastly greater than it was before recordings were available. But that this increase in the number of hearers is necessarily accompanied by an over-all raising of the level of taste does not, in my opinion, follow. In fact, I am convinced that the number of those who listen with joy and with depraved taste to music to which we can ascribe no lofty character, has increased at an equal pace with the listeners to so-called "good" music. I believe that, with some such reservation as was made in the last paragraph, the catalogues and the sales sheets of the recording companies would bear me out. A new invention of the kind we are considering will not, after all, greatly change our fundamental human nature.

But that we are undergoing a significant change in the actual character of our musical life and of our musical civilization must be evident to every serious thinker and observer. This brings me to the point which I should like to make very emphatic as I close this discourse. The age of change in which we are living will appear in history as one of radical revolution in the development of musical life. Living as we do in the midst of the change we are ourselves changing with the new conditions, and we do not become so conscious of their significance. Nor can we see them as clearly as they will stand out to the historian in the future. Their real import and their value to the human race we can only imagine or guess.

Such far-reaching developments in the state of civilization can be observed in past history. Two of them, at any rate, are worthy of attention on this occasion. One of them took place so long ago that we can no longer recognize the details of the actual process. Yet it was, and is, of tremendous significance to the human race. I think of the invention of the art of writing. How vast a difference between the culture that knew no art of communication by written symbols and the civilization that could give permanence to its thought by written records. So far as we know now, we cannot date this art back further than about six-thousand years.

Another radical change in our civilization was brought about by the invention of printing. This happened only five-hundred years ago. The invention is now hailed as one of the triumphs of civilization. I have remarked that the art of recording was being used for the spread of less desirable forms of music as well as in a more ideal direction. It is interesting to note that some serious thinkers bring a similar accusation against the art of printing. The French historian, Jules Michelet, utters a scathing denunciation of those who in the beginning used the new art of printing for the continued propagation of useless medieval ideas and for futile theological comment and dispute, instead of encouraging the printing of the world's great literature.

What would our world be like today if men had never learned to write or if they could not print? The practice of recording sounds will mean as much to mankind. Even though we ourselves stand in the midst of the beginning of the change, it behooves us to become aware of what is really happening, and to contribute our own share to the promotion of every good feature of the new life. Happy are the composers and the performers who live in this age of liberation from the limitations of the fleeting, momentary character of their utterance under the old conditions. Happy are the critics, who need no longer be hampered by the same limitations. Happy are the men and women who are privileged to live through this dawn of a new musical world.

THE EQUIPMENT OF THE MUSICAL JOURNALIST

Paul Henry Lang

I MUST confess that I was somewhat embarrassed by the topic assigned to me by the organizers of the Symposium. When occasionally I venture into the arena of our actual musical life I am scarcely accepted as a member of the critical fraternity, and am usually reminded that professors of music—let alone musicology—are a menace to the well-being of the musical *res publica*. Nevertheless, an invitation from the Music Division of Harvard University amounts to a command performance, and I shall try to tell you what tools I think a musical journalist's workshop should contain.

To begin with, let us dispel an old misconception: criticism is an art, not a science. This does not mean that an artistically written review is at once the equivalent of a good poem or sonata. There are very good reasons, as we shall presently see, why this cannot be so. If we should compare the various types of imaginative writing to a ray of light broken into its components by a prism, the critic's writings would be toward the edge, the ultraviolet rays. On the other hand, criticism without some measure of scholarship is seldom successful, although it must be admitted that occasionally some of the ablest criticisms were written by men who had no musical training, but—and this is of paramount importance—they were eminent men of letters, with a rich humanistic background. No, criticism is not a science based on scholarship alone even though there are criticisms which, like a biological law or the engineering of a piece of machinery, lose their validity the very instant a new, better solution takes their place. As a matter of fact, criticism and scholarship in the respective fields of art are the two faces of a Janus head; they look in different directions but cannot exist without each other.

The critic is a man who sees life in a work of art, a man in whom the spiritual content of a work of art becomes an experience of vital force. This experience acquires in his writing a life of its own, it becomes a profession of faith, a point of view. The critic makes his own the attitude toward life which brought forth the sensation, and endeavors to recreate, in his imagination, the questions the artist asked. This is a mystic and intimate identification during which the internal and the external, the soul and the form, content and expression, unite miraculously; a mystic instant not unlike that moment in tragedy when the hero and his fate become one and the same. As in all true and profound syntheses there is a utilitarian element present. Those experiences the expression of which prompted the critic's writings are not easily shared by others. They are consciously felt in the mind and the mood of most people only during actual contact with the work of art. Even then they seldom show sufficient intensity to impress with their life-giving qualities. Therefore it is only natural that to most people the writings of a critic are mere articles of reporting and elucidation written to inform us about what goes on in the world, to facilitate our understanding, or to help make up our minds for us. There is a profound irony in this. The true critic interprets life and its aims, and yet he speaks of music, books, or paintings as if they were the mere ornaments of this life. It is this ironical circumstance which gives the great critic's writings that wisdom, humor, and force that is so strong that it must not be mentioned, for he who does not notice it will not discern the irony even if underscored.

As we have said, the critic speaks of works of art. What is his relationship with that of which he speaks? The saying goes that the critic must always speak the truth, whereas the creative artist is not bound by such an axiom. But sincerity and inner truth are seldom missing in a great artist. The difference is rather that criticism treats of what has already been formed and by its very nature does not create new things out of nothing, it only rearranges something that already exists. And since it only orders and arranges and does not create a new shape from some raw material, it is bound to it, it has to speak the truth, facts. Or, in a more condensed form, we might say that art takes motifs from life while criticism uses art for its model. "Model" is a word that will lead us to another useful comparison, for the paradox of criticism is almost identical with the paradox of portrait painting. If we view a landscape we never ask whether the painted river or mountain actually bears resemblance to the original models, yet when we look at a portrait the question of resemblance, the literal and superficial application of which is the despair of all true artists, will inevitably arise. We stop in front of a Rubens portrait and say "what a true likeness!" and we are convinced that we have pronounced an artistic judgment. Likeness of whom? We have no idea of the person it represents and yet we still think that the picture resembles the model. There are, then, pictures—and the great portraits are of this sort—which besides other artistic suggestions and sensations give us the life of a man who once lived, and force upon us the belief that this life was such as the painter's lines and colors make us see it. There is a struggle for resemblance, for similarity to the living man's likeness; but it is much more than that. Even if the portrait actually resembles a man at a given time, there are a thousand other occasions when he looks different, when he *is* different. This is the problem of criticism also, its own problem of resemblance and truth, for it too struggles constantly for truth, for the representation of life that the critic espies in a man, a period, or a work. It will depend on the intensity and wisdom of his critique whether he can create the illusion of life, of resemblance and verisimilitude. It is here that the great difference between creative artist and critic resides, because the creative artist conjures up the illusion of life in his creation, while the critic's portrait is an image which can be referred to a concrete model, and therefore this life has to be reconstructed convincingly enough to create an illusion. Yet the task is neither light nor in its own way inferior to the creative artist's task. We cannot accept one man's reconstructed portrait as final and then measure it by the original. We do not measure the real Bach solely with the Bach of Spitta, or of Schweitzer, or of Pirro. Like Saul finding his kingdom while in search for his father's donkeys, the true critic in search of truth will find at the end of his road what in every art is the equivalent of resemblance.

Creating a convincing illusion of life! You may ask whether I intend to make this the chief requisite in the equipment of the music critic. I would do so, but the title of my address is explicit—Harvard University demands that I deal with the musical journalist. Musical criticism and musical journalism can be, but usually are by no means synonymous. There are a few instances when a musical journalist is a true critic, but on the whole musical criticism in our newspapers and periodicals is so far removed from the realm of arts and letters, so inferior to literary and art criticism, that any discussion of its needs must perforce begin with the most elementary requisites. We should begin, then, with the simple equipment of a practical musician. But I am already ahead of myself, for among our critics there are few musicians. A musician is not necessarily a person who can play a Paganini concerto at the drop of a hat or compose a symphony faster than Miaskovsky; but he should be able to read a score, and what is more important, hear it. He ought to be a man who at one time or another went through the holy sensation of moving four parts along the staves, such motion resulting in a piece of music that makes sense. This is not much to ask, but it is the surest way to instill wholesome regard in the mind of the would-be critics for those whose similar exercises result in music that does not immediately make sense to everyone. It takes enormous experience and a highly trained ear to listen to a new symphony or quartet and to form a sure enough opinion of it for the critic to be able to leave by the middle of the last movement in order to peck out in time a review for the morning edition of his paper.

Now, to do justice to the harassed critic, this state of affairs is not of his choosing, it is a routine dictated by journalism. No wonder, then, that those among the critics who never had the benefit of a thorough musical education cannot do justice to their assignment. I shudder at the thought of what would happen to our critics if they had to cope with the customs of the eighteenth century when the public demanded and obtained new works on all occasions, when an opera ran for a few performances and was succeeded by a new one. And at that, his eighteenth-century colleague was very little concerned with the performance—he discussed music.

This brings us to another of those basic reasons, or rather practices, that distinguish the musical journalist from the music critic: he must be a reporter and he is really more concerned with the recreative artist than with the creative. This is in the nature of newspaper work, they say in their defense, but what about the other critics, those of literature, drama, and art? While it is true that, with the exception of the drama critic, they do not have to deal with performance and performers and the hullaballo that surround opera and concert hall, they could still spend columns on trivia. It is to their credit that they are much more professional and serious about their business than their colleague of the music column who, willy-nilly, must write a front-page article on the opening night of the Metropolitan Opera House. This is, of course, a so-called social event and rates the front page. A new symphony or opera of our most distinguished composers never attains this eminence. There is a way, however, for the composer to make the headlines and it usually happens at the opening of the Metropolitan, an event that is not complete without one of those amiable music lovers, who spend the second act at Sherry's on the second floor, losing a diamond necklace. This puts Delibes on the front page, a rare honor. The truth is, of course, that our musical life, concert and opera, is a huge industry combined with the amenities of ridiculous and long-outmoded social conventions. The critic, so it seems, has to conform to these conventions, and there are few of them who dare to dissent. It appears, then, that a good musical training alone is not sufficient to produce a good musical journalist, he has to be something of an independent thinker too.

Before we take up the critic as thinker we must touch upon another purely musical aspect of his equipment: his knowledge of the musical literature and the literature about music.

It is a well-known fact, as earlier speakers have pointed out, that the music industry, like all well run industries, has established a manufacturing code known as the "standard repertory." Mr. Thomson wittily refers to this repertory as the "fifty pieces"—we note that while in literature the rock-bottom requirements call for a "hundred books," in music half that many works suffice. In New York City, where a number of great orchestras converge, it is not unusual to hear the same Brahms symphony or the second *Daphnis and Chloe* suite three times within a week. The performance is, of course, duly reviewed every time in a standard manner with standard epithets, only the respective conductors receive different treatment as befits different personalities. I remember an instance some years ago when *Tristan* was presented during the season six or seven times, and with the same performers. Every performance rated a full column each time. It was during this very same season that a new string quartet by one of our most distinguished composers was barely mentioned by the so-called second-string critics assigned for the occasion. Only one New York critic was aware of his duties and responsibilities in a manner commensurate with the occasion. Well, again, this so-called standard repertory is not of the critic's making; it is the result of business expediency and artistic and mental indifference. But it is up to the critic to protest and bring about a change. However, he can do so only if, unlike the conductor, he knows the repertory that is not standard. The shelves of our music libraries are crowded with hundreds and hundreds of volumes containing great music, why should we deprive ourselves of all this treasure? It would be inconceivable to restrict the art-loving public to paintings of the romantic era with a few eighteenth century and early twentieth century worthies thrown in, and I don't think that I have to carry the parallel into the field of literature. The situation is really nothing short of scandalous and would be so considered in any other field. Some of our eminent conductors subsist on three-dozen works, adding sparingly to their repertory a few pieces, many of which will never be repeated. When the rest period comes and a guest conductor takes over, they veto every piece submitted by the visitor that cuts into their own standard repertory. Since the guest conductor's own repertory is equally limited and contains all the chestnuts that constitute the regular conductor's staples the poor fellow is really in a quandary and is actually reduced to learning some new scores, or rather scores new to him. By studying this vast musical literature the critic could effectively raise his voice, and if he is persistent enough his admonition and counsel would be heeded. But there are other weighty reasons for the diligent study of the literature. Music is not synonymous with the standard repertory; those great masters whose few works like miracles dropped from heaven are links in a long chain of musical events. They themselves have many other works—there are more than three or four symphonies by Haydn or Mozart, to mention one instance—and they have many great colleagues the very names of whom are unknown to critic and conductor, fiddler or pianist. The notion that music really got under way with Bach is still firmly ingrained in most people's minds, but even during the time of the interregnum between Bach and Beethoven we can count on our fingers the works that are in the repertory. Again, to mention one instance, judging from the performances one would never realize that Handel wrote a few dozen oratorios besides the *Messiah*.

We can never really understand the great masters unless we know the soil and the surroundings they grew from. I am prepared to exonerate at least partially the critics' lack of equipment by laying the responsibility squarely at my own doorstep. It is in school that one's interest toward music is aroused and the habit of constantly expanding the musical horizon is formed. Music education is sadly antiquated and stagnant. With some laudable exceptions, we too teach the standard repertory, dressing it up with the time-honored canards and misinformation that is remembered by the critic when he is out on his own. One can hardly blame him when he maintains that Haydn invented the symphony, that fate knocks at the door of the Fifth Symphony, that Schubert, poor soul, never got beyond the second species in counterpoint and could not write good instrumental music anyway because all his things sound like songs, that Brahms could not orchestrate, and that Wagner or Berlioz invented the leitmotiv. Well, they learned these gems from us, but there is a remedy and there is no excuse for the critic not to resort to it. The remedy is the study of the literature on music. Besides containing those endless rows of scores our library shelves are crammed full of books, of good books. It is incredible how little most of our critics read (after all they are, or are supposed to be, men of letters), and how poor the stuff is they do read. A book or art critic would not last long with such a literary equipment. It is true, of course, that much of this literature is in German, French, or Italian, but after all, the critic does not have to practice the fiddle or the piano hours on end, his profession, the profession of letters, demands that he be a student of the relevant literature. The great critics of the nineteenth century were all eminent students of letters and, at the risk of drawing a broadside from the anti-professorial element, not a few of them were excellent musicologists. It would be amusing, if it were not really an example of touching naïveté, that a New York critic, a sworn enemy of musicology, has just come across the name of Lionel de La Laurencie, a distinguished French musicologist who at the opening of our century was already a widely known authority. (Incidentally, this important information was furnished to him by one of his correspondents.) In his mid-sixties at the time when

I was a student in Paris, twenty-odd years ago, La Laurencie was a friend and mentor of his younger colleagues and we never missed the Monday afternoons when he held open house, discussing music. Needless to say, every serious student, however young, is acquainted with La Laurencie's works—he has to be—and if our critic gets around to making use of his discovery and will read those fine works he will be a happier man and will learn a great deal about music.

A little while ago I mentioned the critic as thinker. This calls for an equipment that is not so obviously needed as a musical training, but which nonetheless is of equal importance. A musical journalist is not a mere reporter, he must offer something beyond quotable clippings for artists' managers. He must be a steward of musical life, and above all he must be a friend and protector of the composer. In the eighteenth century a critic was wholly absorbed in music itself, indeed, especially in the earlier part of the century, the musicians themselves were the critics. They scrutinized each other's works, and although feuds and denunciations were not uncommon, as a rule they had respect for each other; and if they grew impatient it was more often than not because they considered a composer too conservative and out of sympathy with contemporary trends. The musicians of those faraway times are usually lamented in the appreciation books for their menial positions, their hard life, and the many restrictions under which they lived. How can we reconcile the incredible productivity of these men with their unhappy circumstances? As a matter of fact, they were neither unhappy nor were they vegetating. A musician in the service of a prince, church, or municipality had relative security of tenure, commissions aplenty, and various incentives—among them frequent performances of his works—to keep on composing. It was only in the nineteenth century, with the so-called emancipation of the artist and the beginnings of modern concert life that his troubles started. True, unlike Haydn, this free artist no longer wore a livery, but he exchanged the picturesque damask frock for an invisible strait jacket, and instead of a prince who commissioned him to write symphonies, quartets, or operas and who sat down to play chamber music with him, this so-called free artist now pays homage to impresario and manager. This new overlord of his does not commission symphonies for he believes only in old and box-officially established ones, and could not play chamber music (for which he does not give a hoot) even if his life depended on it, because his connections with music are solely for business purposes. There were impresarios in the past centuries too and they had to make a living by their business just like their present-day confreres, but they knew a great deal about music, and, curiously, liked it. A man such as Solomon immortalized his name by commissioning Haydn to write a set of symphonies. I wonder whether in the nebulous future there will be occasion to refer to "Judson Symphonies"? We do, of course, see Mr. Judson as a "man of distinction" holding a glass of delicious Lord Calvert whisky, but that again shows that he is appreciated as a shrewd businessman and not as a patron of the arts.

The impresario was not the only one to place himself between artist and public; the virtuoso, who also became an institution in the nineteenth century, stands athwart the other exit. In older times composer and performer were as a rule one and the same person, but in modern times the composer is at the mercy of his interpreter and the manager. With the growth of the music business the composer's role in the hierarchy of the industry has shifted to the bottom of the roster; he is merely an accessory, used if convenient, but most conductors seldom bother to ascertain his wishes if they deign to perform one of his works. This is a humiliating and most harmful state of affairs, and one that is unfortunately aided and abetted by the critics. The result of this attitude is that vast numbers of people go to concerts not to hear certain works but to hear certain performers; they are even willing to listen to a new American symphony if their favorite is conducting. This is where the critics should rise in wrath, but they remain silent— that is, most of them. They are equally silent when it comes to the ridiculous practices in the running of our musical institutions. This great country of ours with its millions of music lovers has one permanent opera house which enjoys a monopoly that Standard Oil could well envy. And all this because of ridiculous social prestige (whatever that means) attached to membership in that august organization. At the same time this old institution is languishing, it has dropped behind the times, and is hostile toward everything fresh and new. There is only one among our leading critics who consistently wars on this antiquated monopoly, most of the others are perfectly willing to accept the *status quo*. The abuses of managers, the concert racket, the shoddy programs, are all properly the critic's concern; he should fight them, and fight them eloquently and with authority; for if the will of the people makes a journalist rather than a critic out of him he should do what all good journalists are doing: speak, and if necessary fight, for the good of the commonwealth, which in this instance is a sound musical culture, within the reach of all.

The gravest and the most serious responsibility of the critic is toward the composer, and this is perhaps where he fails most lamentably. In our present musical life everything is lavished on the performer and little is left for the composer. This makes the city of music resemble a city filled with pedestals with no statues on them. Many a critic (and many a musicologist) labors under the delusion that he outranks the composer, that the latter exists merely to supply him with needed raw material. Such contempt as is shown toward the composer nowadays would have been unthinkable a hundred years ago when people still had reverence for creative genius. Our composers are seldom treated as serious artists who create according to their honest convictions and talents. Instead they are looked upon as intruders in a well-established game and are consequently always measured against the trade-marks long since registered in general esteem. They are constantly compared with the great of the past—to their detriment. Such an attitude is indefensible, and is often degrading. One of our New York newspapers recently published a review of a piano recital in which the critic—a young one at that—had this to say about a new piano sonata: "Well, it won't displace the *Appassionata* in future concert programs." Similarly, a new American opera performed for the first time in the Metropolitan during the past season was greeted with critical catcalls that almost gave the impression that the critics were lying in wait for the poor composer, that they were pleased not to be disappointed in their expectations. Neither the piano sonata nor the opera was a masterpiece, but neither were they the work of impostors. Their composers are serious and able musicians who deserve some measure of respect. How in the name of heaven will they ever write a successful sonata or opera if they are not put through the crucible of actual performance? The composer so rebuked by the critics is very much like the unsuccessful presidential candidate, whom his party will seldom if ever renominate. The unsuccessful opera composer will be seldom if ever again admitted to the Metropolitan's repertory. In Italy and Germany they perform dozens of new operas every year; if the work is not successful they discard it eventually, but no one will dismiss the composer as incurable. The public and the critics will remain in stony silence, or perhaps they will even whistle lustily, but they will always accord the man a second chance, in fact any number of chances. They respect the composer's estate and are usually willing to listen to him again. They know that he has learned his lesson and his next work may be the better for it. Let the unkind American critics look into the writings of those nineteenth-century composers who were also critics: they will discover that with a few exceptions these men —the leading composers of their time—exhibit a genuine concern toward their fellow composers, a careful, even gentle, solicitude toward their musical well-being. And if they peruse these old critical comments they will also discover that the critic of old did not restrict his activity to works actually performed, he reviewed regularly and extensively newly published scores that had not yet been and perhaps were not to be performed.

As I have said, many of our critics are not rightfully admitted to the ranks of the practitioners. They may be well-meaning and honest, but their equipment and training rules them out of bounds in arts and letters. That this should be the case is less the fault of the critics themselves than of the publishers and editors who fail to accord music criticism the dignity it deserves. A man engaged almost at random may turn into that well-known new phenomenon whom we might call the musical surveyor, who always measures, to a fraction of an inch, the distance of the microphone from the singer's larynx, or the decibel juggler to whom musical quality revolves with the surface noises and scratches of the phonograph disk. He may of course turn into a bona fide critic. After a while he gets used to his new profession and the public gets used to him. But we do have some fine critics and I should like to describe at least one of them in order to furnish a concrete example of the intellectual estate of the critic I have tried to establish. I shall talk about a man who represents the ideal, but is no longer active as a newspaper critic, who has a world-wide reputation and is *hors concours*—therefore I shall not get into trouble with any of our musical factions. I am speaking of Alfred Einstein, our distinguished colleague from Smith College, but once the seasoned music critic of the leading newspapers of Munich and Berlin.

Alfred Einstein's debut as a critic and writer on music dates from the first years of our century. The radius of the circle of his experiences reaches back through the last decades of the nineteenth century, while the decisive impressions of his youth came from the transition that marks the opening of the twentieth century. As we all know, this transition era was a battlefield, noisy and merciless. He was in the thick of it, but his voice seemed, from the very beginning of his career, to have a quiet, sober, and honest tone amid the tumult. The threads leading to our immediate ancestors ran through his mental nerves. Every new movement seeks ancestors, but these it seldom finds among its immediate predecessors because the battle is usually fought between neighboring generations. This is the reason why a critic of Einstein's type presents such an interesting portrait of a writer, for he received his first formative impressions from the rear guard of the departing artistic era at the same time when he became aware of the presence of the scouts of the new current. These were the impressions that opened his view into the rich fields of music, and it was from this double perspective that his first writings and critical comments issue. From the very beginning, his horizon was broader than that of his fellow critics, hence the absence of big words. He weighs the issue calmly, his judgments show an unbiased security, he can look into the future. Occasionally he says less than one would expect, because he guards against self-delusions. Thus he becomes doubly useful in bringing new composers nearer to those who, like him, are already saturated with other musical experiences. His tone is mature and re-assuring, backed by solid musicianship and a profound knowledge of the world of arts and letters, it has none of that exaggerated voice of self-imposed leadership which wants to dictate to the composer's pen, nor is it the kind that, filled with its ready passions, occasionally manifests its newness by demolishing the old.

One might say that there are two types of critics, two main types that seem to reappear in every epoch of art. The activity of one of them is closely connected with some artistic movement. The critic of this type receives his aesthetic experiences from the movement and his principles are almost for "home use" only. He is bel-

ligerent and argumentative, as if he would precede the
work itself. He paves the way for new creations. At
times he is born before the new movement, but is often
the product of the new movement itself which rears him
in order to elucidate and further the cause, or even to
close triumphantly the creative path of an artistic epoch.
This type of critic can be of the highest order even
though much beauty will be beyond his horizon; nevertheless, what he absorbs is illuminated by the rays of a
rich soul.

The life of the other main type of critic revolves not
so much around composers as around music. It is
educated by internal discipline. He is at home in all
the warring camps and watches the adversaries closely.
He is usually brought up during a period of transition
and his temperament carries him from one intellectual
territory to another, from which he returns with a more
comprehensive view. He avoids beautiful fallacies and
he does not want to make a mistake even through natural
parti pris. He himself is not a warrior like his cousin of
the other type, therefore his judgments are always reliable for they are rendered away from the battlefield. The
other type loves musical works as if they were his own
creations, at times it seems as if he would glory in himself when speaking of a favorite composer. He likes
to forge virtues from weaknesses, and errors acquire
a new beauty through his enthusiasm. Compared to him
the second type may appear to the untutored or superficial reader as a critic who does not say enough and

who does not really love with ardor. They cannot believe that it is possible to love with such a quiet and
distinguished voice. And yet he too shows all the unmistakable signs of a true lover of art: he likes to speak
of his favorites, but he never speaks of them as if everything about composer and composition has been settled
for eternity and all one has to do is to indulge in paeans.
Since he knows many other territories he can always
measure and compare, he can always find new and interesting facets. It stands to reason that the two types
cannot always be sharply separated, but they are usually
distinguishable. Alfred Einstein belongs to the second
type of critic. When I glanced through his old writings
in the *Berliner Tageblatt* I was vividly reminded of the
critical writings of Flaubert. Like the great French man
of letters, when Einstein discusses a creative artist he
likes to probe not only into the point of view that
prompted the composer's message, but also into the state
of mind of those to whom the message is addressed.
Behind his quiet, at the same time keen and witty, in-
vestigations there is a genuine devotion to music which
lends a warmth to every word.

I suppose that at this point I am expected to suggest
some constructive means to improve the level and
status of music criticism. While I think that the proper
man with the proper equipment and training will take
care of this automatically, and a number of our critics
are such men, I might say that musical taste and a true
appreciation of art would gain if our critics could break

with the routine established by modern journalism and forego the potpourri of reporting and serious art criticism. While there might be some justification in the custom of giving the public a detailed listing of the six concerts given last night, it can be done by other staff members. They will have no difficulty discoursing about the same Bach-Busoni transcription or Kreisler's lollypops for the fiddle that begin and end every piano or violin recital, and Philip Hale took care of the rest. The critic should concentrate on one or two significant works and deal with them in detail. But in order to do justice to both the composer and himself he must find a way to look at the score in advance of the performance and preferably attend a rehearsal or two so that he will be really acquainted with the work by the time he commits his judgment to paper. He should not be afraid to allocate his column to a new overture by Hindemith or Piston, or to a little-known one by an earlier composer even if the rest of the concert is devoted to the First of Rachmaninoff and the Second of Sibelius. And he should never forget that a good song or a good string quartet can be as great as the mightiest symphony. After all, in our day the concert industry in our great cities makes such demands on the critic that it is impossible to do justice to its sheer bulk; as a consequence criticism suffers from the daily monotony of its forced abundance, and from lack of selectivity.

The critics' lot is never enviable. The least enviable among them is, however, the one who never permits his competence to become the plaything of his passions and humors, but always watches out for the judiciousness of his verdicts and for the soundness of his critical credit. He is the one who prefers to love his artistic friends rather than overwhelm them with praise, who does not use his critical weapons for vain and irresponsible bravura to obtain facile and momentary success. And yet how easy it is to play the game of tripping or to bestow fulsome praise. It is as easy to convert the noblest composition into a scandalous offense against good taste as it is to lift to the skies that which time will soon drop into the abyss of oblivion. There was perhaps no era that reckoned with critical success as does ours, which consequently needs conscientious and responsible guides and arbiters. The high order of artistic life is not solely determined by the creative and re-creative artists, it must have its observers and appraisers. But they must remember that the work of art they scrutinize and discuss offers many other problems besides purely artistic ones, and another important thing to remember is that these works are mirrors which almost always reflect the visage that peers into them.

THE FUTURE OF MUSICAL PATRONAGE IN AMERICA

Huntington Cairns

OUR RESPECT for science and art is proverbial. Nevertheless, the majority of men in those fields who devote themselves exclusively to creative work are unable to earn a living. In order to support themselves scientists and artists in general turn to teaching; composers may perform, but the only other occupation which appears open to painters and sculptors in their fields is the production of the "society portrait." For composers the vocations of teaching or performing seem to have no ill effect upon creative work. But the case of the painter and sculptor may be different. If they deflect their energy to the production of "society portraits" they may find in the end that their ability to do conscientious work has been deflected at the same time. When Monet was told that Sargent had announced that he would accept no more commissions for portraits he merely remarked, "It is too late, isn't it?" It is true that the composer, with whose special case we are here concerned, can also turn to potboiling. In fact, it has been argued that the composer should consider, in addition to the usual vocations of teaching, conducting, and the writing of musical criticism, the possibility that the production of potboilers might be a lucrative form of employment. It is thought that since composers such

as Wagner may engage in practices of commercial dishonesty without detriment to their work, they may
also indulge without harm in artistic dishonesty. This
view would have more plausibility if it were not for the
unhappy rule that the artist in any field who deliberately
resorts to shoddy work to earn a livelihood soon loses
an indispensable ingredient of creative activity—the
faculty of self-criticism. The result is that his creative
and commercial productions gradually approach each
other in quality and finally merge at a level nearer the
latter than the former.

In any event, we are confronted in the United States
with the apparent fact that not a single composer is
able to subsist by his serious work. We are also faced
with the fact that in the effort to solve problems created
by the impact of industrialism and democracy upon our
society the form of economic life in the United States is
in a process of transformation. It is held out to us by
the most temperate thinkers that the society of the future will be a reasonable anarchy established on a
broad collectivist basis. By this is meant that the common
means of subsistence will be organized centrally, as in
the present-day distribution of water and electricity; at
the same time the sphere of individual freedom, so far
as it involves the human personality, is expected to be
enlarged. History is full of surprises, and it is possible
that we are tending towards a reconciliation of in-
dividualism and centralization. Meanwhile, it is apparent
that the national income of the United States will not in

the future be distributed as it was in the nineteenth and first part of the twentieth century. Certain sources of income, such as that derived directly and indirectly from wealthy patrons, to which the composer frequently appealed in order to subsist, may no longer be available.

With the rise of industrialism the composer has been confronted with problems which are novel in the history of music. Industrialism means, among other things, mechanical production. For the first time in the history of the world music has become a commodity which is available to everyone at little or no cost. It is manufactured and distributed by the same mass-production methods that have been applied to more tangible commodities. Through the gramophone, radio, and moving picture it is brought to every person. Industrialism appears able to do everything with music except to create it, and since the machines which produce it never tire, the composer is faced not only with an insatiable demand, but with the most numerous audience he has ever encountered. At the same time the composer, in the nature of things, cannot take full advantage of the industrial process. In reality, he belongs to an earlier form of economy from which there is no possibility of escape. He is in the stage of handicraft production, and there he must remain. He is the weaver at the hand loom, and his production obeys the law of "constant cost." The actual hand loom can be supplanted by industrialism with the power loom, and within limits the more the power loom produces the cheaper the cost of the product. But the composer must continue to labor at the handicraft stage although his product, once it has been created, is reproduced and distributed with all the resources of industrialism.

Nothing is more illustrative of the plight of the composer than a consideration of the remuneration that he actually receives. From the smaller orchestral and choral societies, recitalists and chamber-music organizations he receives nothing. An orchestra with a budget of about $600,000 will assign approximately ½ of 1 per cent for royalties. Thus a composer whose work is played by a major symphony orchestra will receive between $20 and $50, provided the composition has not been previously published, in which event the fee must be divided with the publisher. If the performance is at a major opera house the composer receives $100 or less. A symphony which took three years to prepare was played by the New York Philharmonic and the performance was broadcast at the same time nationally by the Columbia Broadcasting System. The composer received a fee of $75. But as he had spent $250 to copy the orchestral parts and for other expenses, he thus suffered a net loss of $175.[1] At a peak period the Philharmonic spent a little more than $900,000 a season. Of this amount $3,500, or less than ⅖ of 1 per cent, was allotted for all the music supplied by composers.[2] A chief problem of in-

[1] David Ewen, *Music Comes to America* (New York: Thomas Y. Crowell Company, 1942), p. 288.

[2] Minna Lederman, "No Money For Music," *North American Review* (Spring 1937), pp. 124–137.

dustrialism has always been that of the unremunerative price. But the present scale of compensation for composers is not chargeable to industrialism. In the handicraft stage, the composer was not able to subsist through his compositions, as the careers of musicians from Palestrina to Beethoven make clear.

In fact, at no time in any society has the serious composer by his own unaided effort been able to count upon a livelihood from his compositions. That is the iron law of music. The composer who pursues a solitary course has always been forced to supplement the income derived from his compositions by the adoption of a subsidiary occupation or the acceptance of patronage. In the language of economics, there has never been an "effective demand" for the serious musical composition. That is to say, the musical composition as a marketable commodity has never been valued in terms that would make its creation an economically justifiable undertaking.

At the beginning of the historical period it is written on the tablets of Nineveh that Sardanapalus was a patron of the arts, a statement from which it may be inferred that even then the arts were not self-supporting. In ancient Greece the composer was a performer, both at public festivals and at the private banquets of the rich; he competed for prizes, and he was commissioned by men of wealth to compose the music for the great public celebrations. With the rise of the Hellenistic world we meet with the first attempt in Greek life to impress a wholly official character upon one aspect of the life of art. Early in the third century B.C. corporate bodies of artists, musicians, and other professionals were organized. These corporations were patronized by the chief cities of Greece and were accorded many important privileges; but even with this help the members were forced to teach as well. Many musicians did not join the professional associations. They earned their living by giving musical performances. In Rome the composers were slaves, or performers, or they were patronized by the rich, or were commissioned by the State, by the managers of the public spectacles, and by ambitious politicians. In the Byzantine world it is the same story. The composer there was supported by the church, the court, or the political factions. With the political support is associated the institution of the double choir singing alternately, one representing the "Blues" and the other the "Greens." During the medieval period the composer of church music derived his livelihood from the church. In the case of secular music, he was a member of a knightly class and was patronized, or he lived upon his income; as a member of a lower class he was a performer either permanently attached to a castle or a wanderer from one musical center to another.

With the Renaissance the account is no different, except that at that time we encounter an exemplar of sound patronage. Two circumstances combined to produce this result. The patron possessed an almost infallible taste, so that he made few or no mistakes in the selection of the persons whom he chose to patronize; his interest in the arts was constant, so that he was ready to acquire all that the artist was able to produce. Thus the artist was confronted with a patron who, while he was ready to support him, could not at the same time be fooled by inferior craftsmanship; moreover, the patronage system of the period assured such a demand for meritorious works that the artist knew he could with security devote himself continuously and solely to creation. At the same time the patron was required to exhibit a measure of physical courage which is not ordinarily associated with patronage. A retainer who had been dismissed might not hesitate to resort to assassination for revenge. However, notwithstanding the ideal characteristics exhibited by Florentine patronage it also possessed some disadvantages, other than the usual dictatorial one which seems inescapable. All artists of any significance found ready support in the Medici; but the Medici could also turn against those whom they helped, as we know from the cry of Leonardo, "The Medici have made me and broken me!" Patronage at its worst we have in the spectacle of a member of the same family employing Michelangelo to carve a snow man in front of his house. More serious is the fact that the artists themselves eventually sought to curry favor with their patrons by indulging what they imagined was their patrons' taste, with the result that the character of the art of the whole period was affected.

By this time the system of royal and private patronage of eminent musicians was well established, although, as we can see in the case of Palestrina, it was far from satisfactory. It could be meagerly remunerative, and dependent too much upon the whim of the patron. Indeed Palestrina's career was not a happy one until he solved his problem by marrying a rich widow. At its best the system of private patronage, which was to persist until the latter part of the eighteenth century, is perhaps exhibited in the person of Prince Nicholas Esterházy, a fair performer himself, and the patron of Haydn. Altogether Haydn was with the Esterházy family thirty years. From the Prince he received every encouragement, and in return he gave a loyalty which forbade him to accept attractive offers of employment elsewhere. What the patronage of the Prince meant to Haydn he has expressed in words which show an acute realization of the advantages which can flow from the patronage system if intelligently administered: "As a conductor of an orchestra I could make experiments, and observe what produced an effect and what weakened it, and was thus in a position to improve, alter, make additions or omissions, and be as bold as I pleased; I was cut off from the world, there was no one to confuse or torment me, and I was forced to become original." [3] But with Mozart the system became intolerable.

Patronage in the long run inevitably associates with itself a social distinction between the patron and the

[3] Quoted in Paul H. Lang, *Music in Western Civilization* (New York: W. W. Norton & Company, Inc., 1941), p. 626.

person who is the object of the bounty. It was upon this rock that the patronage system which had flourished from the sixteenth century foundered in the latter part of the eighteenth. As the Concertmeister at Salzburg of the Archbishop Hieronymus, Mozart was permitted to live in the palace, a distinction not allowed singers and performers. His status, however, was actually that of a personal servant; and since the seating at meals, in accordance with eighteenth-century custom, was formally correct, his place was between the personal valets and the cooks. Inasmuch as Mozart's name for his patron was the *Erzlümmel* (Archbooby) it appeared unlikely that his prospects would be advanced. Seizing upon an incident of no significance in itself Mozart departed from the household of the Archbishop to earn his way as a free-lance artist. It was the end of the patronage system and the beginning of the system we know today.

The road which Mozart opened proved a hard one. He himself was always in want. It has often been observed that Beethoven, while of the opinion that there were many princes but only one Beethoven, continued to accept their patronage and even the benefits of a private subscription; Schubert was always in want; only the intervention of the mad Ludwig II of Bavaria made it possible for Wagner to have his Festspielhaus at Bayreuth. From the *Memoirs* of Berlioz we learn something of the daily hardships of the composer: "Not one among the many millionaires of Paris would ever entertain the idea of doing anything for good music. We do not possess a single good public concert-room, and it would never enter into the head of one of our Crœsuses to build one . . . To be a composer in Paris one must rely on oneself, and produce works of a serious character having no connection with the theater. One must be content with mutilated, incomplete, uncertain, and consequently more or less imperfect performances, for want of rehearsals for which one cannot pay." [4] But the final result of Mozart's revolt, if it did not secure a livelihood for the composer, at least gave him a free hand. The patron might continue to commission works, but he no longer dictated their contents.

In the situation in which the composer finds himself today his plight differs in nowise from that of other creative artists. It is, for example, impossible for the serious or scholarly writer today to support himself by his writing. The learned journals as a rule do not pay for contributions, and the books of such writers, which ordinarily require two to three years' preparation, will sell from twelve hundred to three or four thousand copies. This means that writers of this sort, if they are fortunate, derive about $1,000 a year from their books. Even worse is the case of the poet, at least before he is firmly established. He must either subsidize in part the publication of his volumes, or they are printed in such

[4] Translated by R. and E. Holmes (New York: A. A. Knopf, 1932), p. 476.

small quantities that the royalties, assuming a publisher generous enough to pay them, would maintain him for scarcely a week. Scientists, artists, musicians, and writers are all faced with the same problem. Inasmuch as their productions do not command a price in the market which will enable them to subsist, they must look elsewhere for support. If, as learned historians now argue, our society is in a "time of troubles," a period of "contending states," and war becomes the measure of all things, the scientist may be favored with special treatment by way of patronage, since upon the success of his productions may depend the survival of the whole society. But apart from this perhaps adventitious consideration, there seems no special reason why the workers in one of these fields should be assisted before those in the others. The productions of the scientist may help to make us comfortable, and help us in our efforts to understand the world in which we live; but those of the musicians, the artist, and the writer make life itself, for some at any rate, supportable. The economic problem of the composer is therefore a general one, and any solution that is proposed should take account of the requirements of all groups with complete equality.

It appears unlikely that any economic system which will be imposed upon us in the foreseeable future will alter the historically traditional position of the composer. That is to say, his productions will continue to fetch an unremunerative price. How, then, is the composer to live? The acceptance of any form of patronage involves difficulties not the least of which is that he who pays the piper calls the tune. If the composer can find the means to support himself he has reached the ideal solution. He is then a free agent to follow as he wishes the prompting of his own genius. But he can support himself only by adopting a subsidiary occupation. If that occupation is a congenial one which makes no excessive demands upon his energy there would seem no harm in the composer following that course. It is precisely the one adopted by scientists, writers, and the bulk of musicians today. For writers it was expressly urged by Coleridge in a famous chapter of the *Biographia Literaria*. On the basis of his own experience he addressed to youthful literati the affectionate exhortation: Never pursue literature as a trade. In a recent symposium of British writers on the livelihood to be derived from the trade of letters, Coleridge's argument that a secondary occupation produced no ill effects was substantiated. There was general agreement that the creative writer should at all costs avoid State patronage.[5] To this solution the general objection has been raised that our artistic productions would then be created by amateurs. That is to say, our paintings would be made by "Sunday painters," and our musical compositions created by composers who wrote more as an avocation than as a profession. But Coleridge speaking for literature, Roger Fry for painting, and Ernest Newman for music, none

[5] "Questionnaire: The Cost of Letters," *Horizon* (September 1946), p. 140 ff.

of whom can be charged with indifference to the ac-
complishments in his field, are unanimous in believing
that it would not be a loss, but a distinct gain. The
amateur, free from the compulsion which a life devoted
wholly to artistic creation inevitably generates,[6] is not
tempted to over-produce or to present the public with
second-rate work merely in order to keep his name before it.

As a means to self-help composers can organize themselves, on the model of the Hellenistic Dionysiac *tech-
nitai* described above, into corporate bodies which would
enforce the system of licensing compositions for reproduction on a royalty basis. We have had in the
United States in the past several abortive attempts at
such organizations, and at present the idea is again being
prosecuted. However helpful such organizations may
be in securing some measure of just financial reward to
the composer it is unlikely that in themselves the organizations represent the complete answer to the problem. They never succeeded in securing a sufficient livelihood for the musicians of the Hellenistic period, and in

---

[6] "Listen," Zola causes the writer in *L'Œuvre*, who is modelled
upon himself, to remark: "work has taken possession of my whole
being. Little by little it has stolen me from my mother, my wife, all
that I love. It is a germ carried inside the skull, that devours the brain,
invades the trunk, the limbs, gnaws at the entire body. At once it
lays hold of me as I jump out of bed in the morning; it nails me to
my desk before I have a whiff of fresh air; it follows me to luncheon,
so that I quietly chew over my sentences with my bread; it ac-
companies me when I go out, shares my plate at dinner, lies down on
my pillow at night."

modern times in Europe, where they have been firmly entrenched for several generations, they have been likewise unsuccessful. No musical composition of any sort can be publicly presented in most of the countries of Europe unless part of the box-office receipts are impounded as royalties. This system has served to increase the income of composers, but until the individual composer has accumulated a backlog of many compositions which are constantly being played, his royalty receipts will not be substantial.

In modern society there remain two probable sources of patronage for the composer—the commercial world and the state. The individual patron will no doubt continue to exercise his beneficent influence so long as he possesses the means to do so; but since economists assure us that interest rates will approach zero and will remain there, and since the tax structure is designed to prevent further accumulation of large fortunes, it is plain that the role of the individual patron belongs to the past.

Commerce and industry are already patronizing the arts and they will probably continue the practice so long as the tax system favors it. If such patronage ever becomes a direct charge on profits it is unlikely that stockholders will permit it to continue. But commercial patronage raises a special problem. Will business firms demand that the art which is patronized assist in some way in the advertisement of the commodity which the firm markets? For a commercial firm to patronize artists as artists and not as advertisers of their products would show a degree of aesthetic enlightenment which is rare in the history of patronage. Even the great Florentine patrons could not refrain from directing the nature of the compositions which they commissioned. It so happens, however, that we have witnessed precisely this form of illuminated patronage. Commercial firms have acquired collections of works of art and have commissioned musical compositions solely from the point of view of their artistic merit. The benefit to the firm comes from the advertisement which the firm receives as a patron of the arts when the pictures are publicly displayed and the music publicly performed. If the firm employs the composer from the point of view of direct advertising there is little or no hope for the composer of serious music. It will be the "singing commercial" that the firm quite properly will want. During World War II for example, the first composer engaged by the United States Treasury to compose a song designed to assist the sale of bonds was a popular song writer.

Both commercial and State patronage, however, are defeated in the end by the same obstacle; the artist must establish his ability to the satisfaction of some authoritative jury. Neither business nor the State can afford to endow all who wish to follow an artistic career. There must be a selection of some kind. Inevitably the selection will be made by those regarded as most competent to judge, that is to say, by those who have already established their reputations in the field. But as a general rule it is the young and unestablished who support the innovations which appear in the life of art, and without which it becomes stereotyped and sterile. What we may expect from official boards is typified by the French Academy which, as has been remarked, is always half a generation behind the current practices. Molière, La Fontaine, Zola, Hugo—all were frowned upon by the Academy. At the same time organizations of that type foster standards which ought to be maintained. But since official boards will be composed of elderly specialists, it cannot be expected that the encouragement they will give to art will be of the kind that will foster that anarchic element without which art ceases to grow. If there is any doubt upon that score we need only look at the forms of art encouraged by governments in the production of their coins, currency, and postage stamps. Even worse is the fact that government boards soon pass beyond a mere conservative attitude to the discouragement of types of art which are in conflict with government policy. In the end, as a glance at recent events abroad will show us, the artist if he is to expect any help at all from the State, must become a political propagandist. At that point we pass from art to advertising.

An eminent philosopher once remarked that all problems are divided into two classes: soluble questions, which are trivial, and important questions, which are insoluble. Unfortunately it appears that the problem of the livelihood of the composer falls in the latter category. It is possible, even likely, that we may expect some form of enlightened patronage from both business and the State in the future. An example of the latter is the newly founded Arts Council of Great Britain which assists through government subsidy musical, dramatic, and other organizations promoting the arts. But the Arts Council, as its late Chairman Lord Keynes observed, is ultimately responsible to Parliament, which must be satisfied with what the Council is doing when it votes it money. "If we behave foolishly," Lord Keynes said, "any member of Parliament will be able to question the Chancellor of the Exchequer and ask why." Are we to expect that present and future parliaments have so grown in wisdom that they will vote money to finance the productions of a new Ibsen or a new Wagner? Only someone endowed with even more than the customary share of optimism would venture an affirmative reply to that question. Meanwhile we can expect from the State a helpful indirect patronage. Through its free educational system it can assure possible composers the necessary equipment for the practice of their profession, and through an enlargement of the system of free concerts, or concerts at which only a modest admission fee is charged, it can help to secure the audience which a composer needs. Today, without the patronage of wealth and taste, we are driven back to Coleridge's words which, modified for the present special case, should be engraved on the first blank sheets of music paper handed the young composer: NEVER PURSUE COMPOSITION AS A TRADE.